Sport-A Prison of Measured Time

Sport-
A Prison of Measured Time

Essays by Jean-Marie Brohm

Translated by Ian Fraser

First published as *Critiques du Sport*
by Christian Bourgois Editeur, Paris, 1976
© Christian Bourgois Editeur, 1976

This edition first published, 1978
© Ink Links, 1978
Ink Links Ltd.,
271 Kentish Town Road
London NW5 2JS

ISBN 0 906133 017 Cloth

The Cover Picture depicts Fanny Blankers-Koen, right,
Gardner, centre and Strickland, left
in the 80 metres hurdles, the Olympic games,
August 4, 1948.

Typeset in 11 point Lectura
and printed by Villiers Publications Ltd.,
Ingestre Road, London NW5 1UL

Contents

Preface

Sport is everywhere. Reading about its various manifestations (football, baseball, athletics, etc.), discussing it, watching it or participating in it directly, all take up more hours of the day, for countless millions of people, than any other activity apart from eating, sleeping or working (which includes child-rearing and housework).

And yet, compared with any other major institution in advanced industrialised societies, sport finds itself in a unique situation. Although acres of commentary on sport are devoted to the journalistic arts of prediction, rumour and gossip, back-up information and straight descriptive reporting, the controversies which do abound are entirely contained within the premises of the sporting activity itself. What there is not is any discussion on the institution of sport as such, except perhaps to call for more money and better results.

This silence is characteristic of even critics or commentators who on other questions have quite radical if not revolutionary views. The only exception is racial discrimination in sport, with spasmodic outcries over cricket or rugby fixtures with South Africa. These apart, radicals and Marxists maintain an almost total, sheepish and, it should be admitted, opportunist silence on sport, dictated, it would seem, by the working class's evident enjoyment of it – a fact which, much more than any risk of state repression, has so far effectively stifled critical voices.

It is to Jean-Marie Brohm's credit that he has tackled the sporting institution and the social, economic and psychological relations it sanctifies and encourages, head on. Not for him any temporary accommodation, any modification of his intransigent critique. For only if such a critique finds an echo, first within the revolutionary vanguard and later within the masses themselves, can change take place in the social practice of sport. The years spanned by the essays in this book have seen the emergence in France of the magazines *Quel Corps* and *Le Chrono Enrayé*, the Anti-Olympics Committee and, more recently, the Committee for the Boycott of the World Cup organised by the Argentinian dictatorship. Brohm has been actively involved in all of these.

Now, it is true that the origins and development of sport are very different in the Anglo-Saxon world than in France. The most obvious is the comparative non-interference of the state in its promotion in the former. Sport's aristocratic origins in Britain, a relaxing pastime for the rich, surrounded by an aura of 'amateurism' which clings to it still, implied a struggle on the part of the working class for the 'right to sport'. This right was all the more readily conceded given the numerous benefits that it provided the ruling class in the form of a more disciplined and healthy working class (and potential soldiery) spending less time on the more politically inflammable pursuits of reading, discussion and self-organisation. Sport became an organic part of society, taken up 'spontaneously' by all classes almost from the cradle to the grave.

Perhaps closer inspection into the conquest of the masses by sporting pursuits of various kinds would reveal a very active intelligentsia – priests, school-teachers, professional people – who played a surprisingly conscious role in this conquest. Baden-Powell and Thomas Arnold were early representatives of this intelligentsia, mainly concerned with cementing the new ruling class block to which they belonged – one was a public school headmaster, the other an army general. With such an intelligentsia whose roots stretched deep into society, the state could play the role of national centraliser and benevolent provider of funds for private initiatives promoting general enjoyment and relaxation. How much more congenial a role to that of the Gaullist régime painted by the *Draft Doctrine on Sport* taken up in the book. But in the end, whether sport assumes mass proportions through the organic development of 'civil society' or through the interventions of a centralising state, once it has established itself as a mass practice, its social role is more or less the same. This role is amply documented by Brohm and it is not the purpose of this short introduction to repeat him. It is worth stressing, nevertheless, that sport is a classical example of an activity which has almost diametrically opposing class implications dependent upon who is actually engaged in it.

For the bourgeois playing amateur sport, the watchwords of the sporting canon – competition, 'grit the teeth', 'fair play', 'team spirit', 'all pull together' etc. – are as self-evident and natural as the air he breathes. Indeed, they *are* his watchwords for life itself. They transpose quite naturally for him from his individual conduct to that of a company or indeed a nation. Here they may take on fancier, more imposing titles: Free Enterprise, Competitive Trading Position, the Dunkirk Spirit, the National Interest, Equality before the Law, etc., but the inherent ideas are the same. For the proletarian, each and every one of these watchwords of sport is a breach in his own class solidarity. Despite sophistical attempts, by some sociologists, to reinterpret them in proletarian renderings, they remain what they are and what they are meant to be: *manifestations of the essence of bourgeois ideology infused into every nook and crevice of social existence under capitalism*, and are to be fought as such.

It is for this reason that it is high time that the fight back against this *opiate of the people* should begin in the Anglo-Saxon world, completely saturated as it is with sporting events, imagery, vocabulary and practice – from the Primary school playing field, to Royal Ascot, from College baseball to the World Series.

Brohm's book is neither a panacea nor a complete whole. The essays which make it up are so many *interventions* into different conjunctures.

Although they very often deal with the same themes, the arguments are not simple repetitions but develop and become more refined or approach the subject from different angles. The *20 Theses on Sport*, at the end of the book, are the distillation of many years' work. The reader will notice that quite a few of the references and quotations supporting an assertion pertain to the situation in France (save for the chapters on the Olympics and East Germany). However, it is not difficult in most cases to recall similar quotations (from journalists, sportsmen and women, sports ministers and bureaucrats etc.) made in Britain, the US or elsewhere, repeating exactly the sentiments expressed by their French counterparts. Rather than encumber the pages with numerous references to English language sources, we hope that the book will encourage some people to prepare similar requisitories on sport in the English speaking world.

Introduction: Enough of the Myth of Educative Sport

This book brings together a number of articles or statements written at different times. All of them were conceived as theoretical *interventions* in particular ideological contexts, as fragments of analysis in concrete institutional situations, which in fact involved taking sides in given national and international political conjunctures. They are intellectual weapons, or to use Mao's expression; 'arrows' aimed at the 'targets' constituted by a range of opposing positions. In this respect we have followed one of the basic principles of the materialist dialectic, namely that theoretical analysis is first and foremost directed against its ideological opposite – a critical negation of the 'positive' represented by the established order of things and above all by the positivism of self-satisfied complacency and common sense.

Most of these essays can be situated in the period following the events of May and June 1968 in France, which saw the barbarous and frenetic offensive launched by American imperialism in Indochina in 1972 and which culminated in the consolidation of a strong state in France, regimented by the ministry of the interior.[1] Against the background of a new rise in militancy in the workers' movement and numerous mobilisations of young people, this period was characterised by an intense ideological debate sparked off by the crisis of bourgeois institutions and values.

The articles are thus *dated* in so far as they reflect the 'Zeitgeist,' the mental climate of this anxious world. In particular they are marked by the rhythms of the Olympics in Grenoble and Mexico in 1968 and in Sapporo and Munich in 1972, and also by

1. On this question, Cf. Brohm, Touvais, Pellegrini, Frank in *Quatrième Internationale*, 'Le Gaullisme, et après? Etat fort et fascisation'. Maspéro, Poche Rouge, Paris, 1974.

a series of confrontations and discussions over sport which took place in the context of public debates or through a collective elaboration in various left wing political, theoretical and trade union reviews. However the articles are not presented in the chronological order in which they were written or published but are arranged so as to show the *progressive unfolding* of their argument. For we consider that analyses of competitive sport and related phenomena should be presented in as *didactic* a manner as possible, since in general the reality of sport constitutes *a huge blind spot* for social consciousness – including intellectuals. Sport acts as a bloc of virulent repressions and it is correspondingly difficult to bring its socio-political meaning and its ideological functions for state monopoly capitalism to the surface. This concern with explanation and clarification partly justifies the inevitable repetitions and the somewhat demonstrative tone of the articles. In this respect we have followed the advice of Lenin as a teacher: repeat, repeat and repeat again.

We consider it necessary to publish this collection of articles today for two reasons. First of all, the book enables us to make a critical survey of a theoretical and political approach shared by an entire current of critical opinion among teachers and students of physical education and sport and, more generally, among those who might be termed the *new 'organic intellectuals'* of the body, to borrow Gramsci's expression. These include all those people directly or indirectly concerned with the 'social practice of the body' – whether physiotherapists, psychologists, re-adaptation specialists, leisure activity leaders, or holiday camp monitors, teachers and so on – who side with the struggle for the emancip-ation of the working class and are no longer prepared to accept the dominant institutionalised forms of bodily development and the traditional practice of physical and sporting activity. The purpose of bringing together a series of texts which have become difficult to obtain, either because they are out of print or because they are scattered among a number of different periodicals, is to be able to assess where we have got to by putting forward a coherent body of propositions.[2] The intention is to map out clearly the lines of force in the field of the critique of sport, to bring out

2. These positions have been developed in the course of a long process of collective work. The issue of *Partisans*, 'Sport, Culture et Répres-sion' (republished in Petite Collection Maspéro, Paris, 1976) was

certain reference points and to outline the various controversies and shades of opinion. It is clear that *the dialectic of an analysis is determined by the positions against which the analysis is developed and asserted.*[3] Thus our critique of state capitalist sport is also a critique of the proposals made hitherto for the reorganisation of sport, whether inspired by humanitarian, modernist, technocratic or reformist ideas. As Marx put it, to be radical means going to the roots of things . . .

Secondly, the presentation of this survey of the different possible approaches to the question aims to bring out, in a way that goes beyond the usual statements of principle, *the urgency and the scope of the theoretical sociology of sport* that is needed – a sociology rather different from a mere empirical catalogue of statistical or quantitative data, anthologies of interviews with leading sportsmen or hymns to the glory of eternal sport with its humanist ideals.[4] The book gives a necessarily limited idea of the

    really the starting point. The work came to fruition in the publication *le Chrono Enrayé* (a supplement to l'Ecole Emancipée) (Cf. in particular the two issues devoted to the Munich Olympics – No. 8, May/June 1972 and No. 9, September 1972.) This work is being continued at present within the framework of the review *Quel Corps?* (1, rue des Fossés-Saint-Jaques, Paris, 75005) which attempts a critique of the status of the body within capitalist social relations and analyses all aspects of the institution of sport with a view to developing alternative forms of physical education in a perspective of the transition to socialism and communism. Finally, mention should be made of the collection entitled *Corps et Culture*, edited by Michel Bernard for Editions Universitaires, Paris: M. Bernard, *le Corps*, 1972; D. Denis, *le Corps enseigné*, 1974; J.-M. Brohm, *Corps et politique*, 1975. A book of collective discussion is shortly to appear in this collection: *Quelles pratiques corporelles maintenant?* All of these works blaze the trail for the challenge to competitive sports and its alienation. For the analysis of the institutional factors in the stifling of young people, in which competitive sport plays a key role, see: M. Field and J.-M. Brohm, *Jeunesse et Révolution*, Petite Collection Maspéro, Paris, 1975.

3. Cf. *Contre Althusser* (collection) Union Générale d'éditions 10/18, Paris, 1974, and most recently (with reservations) A. Badiou, *Théorie de la contradiction*, Maspéro, Paris, 1975.

4. There are already several books in France dealing with the phenomenon of sport, or at least with certain of its aspects. Most of them however have serious defects of method which render their conclusions unconvincing. Among the ideological and epistemological presuppositions involved in their approach are the following:
    – the belief in a timeless 'eternal sport'. There is held to be a historical continuity from the ancient Greeks to the present day, sport thereby being considered over and above modes of production. Sport, thought to be as old as the hills, is thus supposed to have remained essentially

tasks facing such a deepgoing sociological investigation. A series of problems remain to be analysed in greater detail: the sports production process; the effects on mass psychology of the spectacle of sports contests – identification with the stars, the concentration and release of impulses etc. – the role of the media, television, the press and advertising, in propagating a sports

the same down the ages, and to reflect unchanging features of 'human nature'.

– The 'ideals of sport' and in particular the 'pure' ideals of the Olympics are held to have been diverted from their initial vocation by various 'excesses', 'abuses' and exaggerations reflecting the passions of our time. This is the thesis which regards sport as basically healthy, but 'deformed' by 'bad practices'.

– The political or ideological corollary of the preceding thesis is the conception of sport as 'confiscated', that is to say the thesis that sport, the systematic practice of physical competition, is neutral and simply used in different ways in different socio-political régimes according to the ideological objectives of one or another social class. This is the conception behind all attempts to place sport at the service of 'humanity', 'socialism' or even 'the revolution', after having separated it from the 'dross' of capitalism or industrial society. This is to forget that *sport is an institution and therefore not a tool which can be put to different uses independently of the social production relations in which it grew up and within which it is reproduced.* By projecting sport into an autonomous sphere, capable of being transferred from one social system to another, today's ideologists of sport, especially those of the French CP, make the same mistake as that which Marx criticised on the part of Proudhon concerning the economic category of property: 'M. Proudhon, in treating property as an independent relation, is guilty of several errors of method, showing clearly that he has not grasped the link between all the different forms of bourgeois production and that he has not understood the historical and transitory character of the forms of production in a given period. M. Proudhon, who fails to see our social institutions as historical products and understands neither their origin nor their development, is only able to put forward a dogmatic critique of them.' (K. Marx, letter to P. Annenkov, 1846.)

A good example of the thesis of 'confiscated' sport can be found in the latest theoretical production of the PCF: the collection entitled *Sport et développement humain,* Editions sociales, Paris, 1975. Guy Besse writes (pages 41 and 42) that 'the big bourgeoisie spares no efforts to take control of this phenomenon for its own profit'. As if the bourgeoisie needed to take control of an institution which has been its own property ever since becoming a ruling class. It is thus not surprising to find the PCF acting as a loyal defender of the bourgeois system, proposing some original slogans: 'The defence of sport against the damage and deformations resulting from capitalist exploitation is a revolutionary task' (p. 27). Doubtless this task is of the same order as the defence of the Gaullist strong state and bourgeois morality against the 'perversions' brought about by a 'handful of monopolies'!

world-view; the function of sports techniques in structuring a social image of the body and their role in the repressive socialisation of psycho-motor behaviour; the values and unconscious fantasies that underlie the mythology of sport played out in the social imagination: tales of fabulous exploits which dramatise the dominant patterns of bourgeois ideology, the list could go on.[5]

The essays focus on *the analysis of élite, top-level competitive sport* since this is the driving force behind mass and leisure sport and is indeed the stimulant of predominant physical activities in general. Apart from the act of labour, the dominant and fundamental way man relates to his body in state capitalist society is through sport – inasmuch as it is through the model of sport that the body is understood in practice, collectively hallucinated, fantasised, imagined and individually experienced as an object, an instrument, a technical means to an end, a reified factor of output and productivity, in short, as a machine with the job of producing the maximum work and energy. And it is precisely this competitive sport and the conception of the body which it exemplifies which have now entered *a period of continuous crisis*.

'Indeed, élite sport, with its diseased structures, has reached crisis point.'[6] This opinion, voiced by a team of journalists, is a clear sign of the present crisis in competitive sport, linked to the crisis of state monopoly capitalism. The crisis of the sports institution is a complex affair and is still developing, but it is already possible to discern some general tendencies which can only be aggravated in the future. The first symptom of the crisis is the fact that sport is being discussed in somewhat less puerile terms than those traditionally employed in official parlance *(mens sana in corpore sano*, etc.) People are beginning to speak out within and about the institution of sport. The analysis of the institution follows a long undermining process. 'Well dug, old Mole!', as Marx would have said. The next factor deepening the crisis in sport is the extraordinary proliferation of diagnoses, not all of which are particularly scientific or critical, which seek to identify the disease and prescribe the appropriate remedies. The decisive fact is that today *the basic consensus has broken down*. Sport can no longer be naïvely treated as a value unaffected by

5. J.-M. Brohm, 'Sociologie Politique du Sport', Edition Universitaires (J. P. Delarge), 1976.
6. P. Georges *et al, Champions à vendre*, Calmann-Lévy, Paris, 1974, p. 8.

the political and ideological class struggle. Sport is now a *central political issue* in the social conflicts of our time. Things can no longer go on in the same old way. No one, at least no one in the politicised vanguard of the workers' movement, among young people or teachers, still falls for the traditional watchwords: Work, Family, Fatherland and Sport. This rise of consciousness is now irreversible and it even extends to some of the sportsmen themselves. Sport, like other institutions, is suspected of propping up the class rule of the bourgeoisie, or of the Stalinist bureaucracy in Eastern Europe. In Hegel's words, sport is slowly subsiding, or even being gnawed away by the thoroughness, the patience and toil of the negative. The language of the sociology of sport is the language of crisis.

The crisis in sport is not an isolated event, but constitutes a not unimportant element of what Trotsky called the general crisis of imperialist decay. Sport's crisis is over-determined by the crisis of bourgeois society as a whole, and in turn it contributes to the deepening of that crisis. The Munich Games in 1972, which marked the explosive climax of what R. Lourau has called the 'institutional trance' affecting sport, brought to light all the economic, political and ideological factors at play in the institution. For a few hours sport was blown to pieces and even reactionary bourgeois commentators were forced to question the purpose of sport.

For some time now the question of the political and cultural significance of sport has been acutely posed. No one can any longer avoid taking a stand. Thus in France, the right wing bourgeoisie openly holds out sport as a means of defending the 'advanced liberal society' which has since become so dear to the heart of president Giscard. In 1971, the editor of *l'Equipe*, a mass circulation daily sports paper, wrote:

> 'Comparing different social systems, it is imperative for nations with what we term liberal régimes *(sic)* to re-think the problem of sport, and indeed to take the clear decision to bring sport into the lives of our peoples, starting in nursery school. If we want to preserve our way of life and keep a system which claims to protect individual liberties, our young people must be provided with the means of strengthening themselves.'[7]

7. *L'Equipe*, 20.9.71.

In other words, a fraction of the French bourgeoisie, scared by growing militancy in the workers' movement and the sharpening of social conflicts which threaten the very survival of capitalist society and which point the way towards solutions to the crisis of western bourgeois culture, is desperately seeking to legitimate and prop up its tottering system, either by turning to the army as the 'last line of defence of liberal society', in the words of defence minister Galley, or else by turning to sport, the *new opiate of the people*.

It is thus no accident that most of the top representatives of the French ruling class are trying to come to grips with the scope and the effects of the crisis in sport. Recently the minister of youth and sport, M. Mazeaud, referred to the challenge to sport as ruling ideology in the following bitter terms:

'We are faced with a new "intellectual" rejection of sport by theoreticians who see sport as a form of human alienation'. He concluded with his view of the root cause of the crisis: 'What then is the real reason for these accusations against sport? Let's not kid ourselves. These accusations are just one aspect of the contemporary crisis of values: one aspect of a fierce argument in which our very civilisation is being challenged.'[8]

Indeed it would be hard to miss the fact that the crisis of sport both refracts and aggravates the general crisis of capitalist society, whether this takes a dramatic or a more insidious form. Along with the army, the family, the education system, the church, the asylums and prisons, justice and the police, the institution of sport could hardly be expected to escape the crisis of bourgeois values and the breakdown of the social consensus.

Similarly the former UNESCO director, René Maheu, in a speech made during the 1972 Munich Games (*Sport in our world – its possibilities and problems*), anxiously noted the developing contradictions between the official ideology and the world-wide practice of sport. Observing the fact that sportsmanship, fair play, the moral and educational virtues and the life-ethic embodied in sport are increasingly negated by the very success of sporting confrontations between states, Maheu insisted on the need for sport to return to its origins: 'to bring out a moral purpose, as

8. *Le Monde*, 1.12.73.

the founder of the modern Olympic games wished,' in other words to bring about an urgent reform of sport.

'It is impossible to deny,' he went on, 'that the development of spectator sport has turned attention away from the moral value of sport for the individual towards its entertainment potential. For the mass of people, sport has become a form of entertainment of which they are mere spectators; radio and television spare them even the trouble of getting to the sportsground. The success of spectator sport and the importance it has come to assume in everyday life are unfortunately too often exploited for purposes alien or even opposed to sport — commercialism, chauvinism and politics — which corrupt and deform it. *If we want to save sport's soul, the time has come to react and react quickly.*'[9]

For governments and sports officials the matter has become more urgent still in that the 'discontents in sports civilisation' inevitably lead to revolt and criticism on the part of its victims, a fact which is sportingly acknowledged by our eminent philosopher of culture: 'Thus we see a section of our young people condemning sport as a source of alienation — *this warning sign should put us on our guard.*'[10]

In fact the institution of sport in France has been in difficulty for some time. The much publicised weaknesses and failings of *our* champions and *our* élite have eventually become a national problem which deeply preoccupies the government. Everything is going wrong. Athletics is short of competitors,[11] football and

9. Quoted in *l'Equipe* (René Maheu, 'L'éducation et le sport'), 27-28.12.75.
10. Ibid.
11. Athletics, as a basic sport, is held to reflect the vitality of a nation. Not only has the objective of 100,000 club members not been attained, but there is at present a decline in the number of people joining the French Athletics Federation and a drift away from this sport. As R. Pointu stressed in *Le Monde* (29.1.76): 'Last year the decline was such (from 92,562 to 87,331) that superficial explanations such as those linking the initial decline to the events of May '68, are no longer being advanced. The rot has set in more and more deeply, affecting progressively younger age-groups'. That is why the Federation is set on winning the favours of junior athletes even if it means 'poaching' the champions of the future from other sports which are also trying to boost their recruitment. As R. Pointu went on to observe: 'It will doubtless be some time before the federations agree amongst themselves to put a stop to the competition for ever younger members — competition described as 'baby snatching' (ibid). For the same reason the sports

professional cycling are in permanent crisis,[12] skiing is in a mess,[13] rugby and basketball are rocked by repeated scandals, international successes are few and far beween and in major Olympic events we come nowhere. In one way or another, every sport is a headache for the national officials. This structural crisis of the French sports system is compounded by the *challenge* to the 'rules of the game' coming from the *participants* themselves. More and more sportsmen are challenging the organisational principles by which sport is governed, the 'oriental despotism', arbitrary rule and internal hierarchy of the federations and clubs, their bureaucratic management and the absence of initiative

minister Mr Mazeaud is considering making athletics compulsory at school, so as to overcome the serious crisis of recruitment and encourage the practice of sport from the earliest age, which is a necessity for spotting and bringing forward the champions of the future: 'Perhaps we ought to make athletics compulsory within the curriculum of studies and physical education. I know that all PE teachers already teach athletics. But I wonder whether this might not be a way of bringing a larger number of young people to practice top-level competitive athletics' (*Le Monde*, 27.1.76).

12. French professional football is going through a period of inflation of players' wages, an absence of a coherent policy for the recruitment of young players, an escalation of the level of the transfer fees paid to retain star players, often from foreign clubs, increases in overheads of every sort and a rough and ready system of financial management, which has led to a number of recent scandals, and which means that most of the clubs are heavily in debt and increasingly dependent on state intervention. The state intervenes, as in the case of regional aid or subsidies to firms in trouble, to finance rationalisations and rescue operations. Given the importance of football as a popular national sport, the state has found it necessary to seek a solution to the chronic crisis of the industry. Despite local authority grants, advertising receipts and gate takings – which amounted to 65 million francs in '74-'75 – the clubs are running up disturbingly big losses. 'The professional clubs are said to have a total overdraft of 40 million francs' (G. Albouy, *Le Monde*, 24.1.76).

13. French skiing is in the dock: the insatiable greed of the 'pool' of official suppliers to the French team; the local rivalries within the French ski federation; the lack of authority of the trainers; the easygoing attitude of the champions; a widespread lack of confidence within the French team; the notorious incompetence of certain managers – the charge sheet goes on growing. Following the Innsbruck games in 1976, the little world of French winter sports lamented: 'It's the worst rout for 40 years . . . what a come-down in such a short time' (*Le Monde*, 17.2.76). This is what lies behind the combined efforts of all the parties concerned to 'clean up the spirit of the French club, which has been more concerned with financial profitability than with sporting achievement' (Ibid.).

allowed to the members. The positions taken by such progressive sportsmen are a reflection of a general tendency in the present period: the demand for the right to control one's own affairs. The institution has even experienced the beginnings of self-management at the base. Other competitors have forcefully advanced economic demands. Conscious of their role as exchange-values, and as perishable commodities at that, they have begun to demand wage rises, increased bonuses and numerous fringe benefits, paid holidays and the right to retire from sport at the age of 35. Unemployed footballers and cyclists are demanding security of employment and improved social benefits.

The most recent illustration of the crisis of authority in French sport was provided by the 'Hara-kiri of French basket-ball', as *l'Equipe* described it (11.3.76). Eleven international players selected for the French team attempting to qualify for the Montreal Olympics were dropped. The players concerned were further banned from all friendly club matches in France or abroad. The reason? They turned up a day late for the pre-Olympic training session held at the national sports institute which had to be cancelled since only 5 out of 18 players were present. This disciplinary measure, out of all proportion to the offence, is a good illustration of the totally arbitrary rule of the bureaucratic sports establishment. The bureaucrats' prime concern is to assert their authority, even if that means resorting to methods worthy of any army sergeant-major. The punitive intention of this measure reflects the reaction of a caste determined to hang on to its power. The president of the French basket-ball federation, R. Busnel, justified the punishment in the following terms:

'We must put an end to this situation of anarchy by punishing this kind of attitude, even if we have to pay a heavy price, for the federation is punishing itself by reducing our chances of qualifying for the Games . . . The decision was taken without passion or anger. There is no question of going back on it before the end of the Games. I take full responsibility for the decision which was needed to restore order.'

L'Equipe justified the federation's reassertion of its authority over the recalcitrant players as follows: 'Above all a principle must be defended in face of the aggressiveness and casual rudeness of young people acting unthinkingly like so many spoilt

children . . . spoilt by their clubs, by their federation and even
by the army. Up till now soldiers have benefitted from special
privileges enabling them to be virtually at the disposition of their
clubs. They could more or less do their national service as
civilians. Their unthinking and indisciplined behaviour has led
to the loss of the advantages they were accorded as sportsmen by
virtue of the services they could render to French sport.'
(11.3.76).

In other words, sportsmen accorded favours, sinecures and
privileges are to be treated as soldiers on duty, punishable for
the slightest slip, breach of discipline or prank. Sports discipline
is modelled on military discipline, with its call-up, roll-calls, troop
inspections, uniforms, punishments, deference to superiors, blind
obedience and overall respect for hierarchy. Even the most integrated of sportsmen are beginning to rebel against this type of
discipline. This in turn leads the institution to react in order to
reassert its authority – the process is already familiar in the
context of the challenge to military discipline in conscript regi-
ments. As *Le Monde* described the situation (12.3.76),

'Breaches of discipline, disrespect for the hierarchy, abuse of
privileges – the time has come to call a halt to such an
intolerable situation! The sports establishment which continues
to treat athletes like ill-disciplined soldiers and lectures them
in a tone that would not even pass in a present day class room,
this establishment speaks of a situation of anarchy, merely
because the authority of a federation is challenged. Certain
commentators, unintentionally revealing the paternalistic treatment accorded to the players, are describing the basket-ball team
as "spoilt children" . . . For a good ten years now, for reasons
best known to themselves, the French basket-ball federation has
pursued a policy of all-out support for the clubs. Over the course
of the decade this amateur sport, once a typical product of local
patronage, has become one of the finest flowers of thinly disguised
professionalism. After deliberately turning these athletes into
wage-earners, the federation should hardly have been surprised
at their lack of enthusiasm for working for nothing. Do the
officials really think they can save face by feigning outraged
innocence and resorting to the language of fifty years ago?'

All the political forces are involved in a race against the clock to save French sport and provide the country once again with a sporting élite worthy of her national ambition. On the right wing, the régime has just passed a law to encourage the development of sport: the Mazeaud Law. The aim is to stiffen the nation's sporting fibre in the schools and universities, in the work-places and in the army. The preamble to the law spells out that 'Because of its importance, sport is an activity of public interest which it is the nation's duty to encourage.'[14]

At the same time, and in the same spirit, the sports establishment is organising 'sports study groups' all over France for all the main sports disciplines. The avowed aim of these groups is to produce top-level athletes capable of holding their own against the international competition: to give France a sports élite which she so sorely lacks when compared with other countries such as E. Germany. 'These sports study groups,' explains M. Mazeaud, 'are the only way to save French sport.'[15] D. Mennesson has observed that 'from the outset, no one could be under any misapprehension: these groups were officially set up with the aim of selecting out a sporting élite so that France could do well in international sports meetings. By considering that they can save French sport merely by ensuring that our champions land a few medals, surely the powers that be are taking a short cut, leaving the mass of school students by the way-side.'[16]

On the left wing the picture is much the same. The French C.P. for instance, has for some years been waging a vigorous campaign against the 'failings of the régime' in the field of sports policy. In this campaign the C.P. lays on sporting nationalism

14. Cf. B. Ramon, 'Towards a critique of the Mazeaud Law', in *Quel Corps?* No. 1, April/May 1975.
15. 'Sports study groups to train tomorrow's champions,' in *Le Monde de l'éducation*, No. 13, Jan. 1976, p. 21.
16. Ibid. p. 21. It is worth noting that the training provided is particularly tough. In swimming for example, girls from 11 to 15 years old train two hours a day in the pool from 5 pm to 7 pm, as well as an hour's training in competitive conditions two or three times a week. An official of the swimming group at the Jeanne-d'Arc secondary school, Orléans, observed: 'Our girls cover five or six kilometres a day in the pool – in E. Germany they do 18.' In the same vein, the leader of the athletics group at the François I Lycée, Fontainebleau, declared: 'To get from national to international standard you need not two hours training a day, which is what we do at present, but four.' In this light it is not surprising to observe 'the astonishing seriousness of these boys and girls who lead a truly ascetic life' (D. Mennesson, ibid. p. 20).

and provincial chauvinism with a trowel, lamenting the lack of success of *our* champions. The C.P.'s sparkling general secretary, G. Marchais concluded a recent interview in the following terms:

'A sports enthusiast cannot help being distressed by the poor results obtained by our national teams. No, it's not the athletes' fault. We accuse the government's sports policy: the lack of finance and the poverty of school sport for which the government has made such feeble efforts. It has to be said: this policy is detrimental in the first place to the physical education of our young people, but also to their mental development. Sport inculcates a fighting spirit and teaches endurance. So when we see France bringing up the rear in international competition, that is further proof that in every field, the time has come for a change of policy.'[17]

Following the 'national catastrophe' of the Innsbruck games the party of 'national unity' and the 'union of the French people', in true populist style, launched a huge operation 'call to arms'. 'One medal out of 121 for the French team at Innsbruck', was *l'Humanité's* headline. R. Passevant's article, entitled 'Tail-end Charlies of the Olympics' went on: 'Once again the games are over and once again nothing has gone right for the French. Anger prevails in the press and on the air. Innsbruck is a hard pill to swallow. During the last fortnight our country has provided the pathetic spectacle of a sports community gone adrift.' The journalist slated the 'crazy sports policy' which 'condemns our young people and our athletes to pick up the discarded Olympic caps . . . and our country to lose prestige, reduced to playing the bit parts.'[18]

In the same vein, Guy Hermier, Political Bureau member and leader of the sports commission of the French C.P.'s central committee started by singing the praises of the 'great success' of the Innsbruck games, the 'high level of the performances' and the 'international impact of the games' ('2 million spectators on the spot and 600 million T.V. viewers make this an event out of the ordinary'). He went on to laud the fact that the games were seen as 'a great demonstration of friendship and solidarity among the peoples and youth of the world' and paid the obligatory tribute

17. *L'Humanité*, 19.8.75.
18. *L'Humanité*, 16.2.76.

14

to the successes of the 'socialist countries such as the USSR and
E. Germany'. Finally he rehearsed the now familiar theme of the
threat to sport from the monopolies, interspersed with the no less
inevitable chorus of sporting chauvinism. 'The failures of Innsbruck
are a sign of big problems ahead for Montreal. The culprit is the
régime's policy. The policy is detrimental to the level of French
sport and thus to our country's influence in the world.' Restating
his conviction that on the basis of the C.P.'s policy 'as recently
reasserted by our 22nd. Congress, France has the potential to
become a great sporting nation', Hermier called on public opinion,
on sportsmen all over France, on parents, workers and young
people to demand the doubling of the Sport and Youth ministry's
budget, the 'development of sport in schools and work-places',
increased resources for the sports movement and the 'democratisation of sport'. 'On this basis', he concluded, 'as a true sports
patriot and apostle of the "Olympic peace", top level sport could
play its true role as a cultural activity, as a spur to progress and
as an agent of international exchange. The élite would no longer
be a product of chance. Needless to say, concrete and specific
measures would be taken to reconcile the demands of sport, work,
studies and the careers of the champions.'[19]

The reality of sport is not as rosy as is often made out. In every
field people are beginning to realise the price paid for success in
the medals race. Everywhere people are wondering about the
human, educational, cultural and political consequences of the
hunt for new records, of the frantic drive for biological output
and of nerve-racking physical challenges. The unease caused by this
painful questioning of sport's perspectives contributes to the
crisis. 'Just how far can top-level competitive sport go? Will not
the many deviations suffered by sport sooner or later lead to its
complete degeneration?' R. Parienté's question[20] highlights all the
internal contradictions of the practice of competitive sport. We
will look at just a few of the recent tendencies which render top-
level sport more and more absurd, bringing sport towards its own
negation.

While educationalists all stress the potential of sport for peace-
making through the bringing together of individuals, peoples and
nations and development of mutual understanding, in fact the

19. *L'Humanité*, 18.2.76.
20. *L'Equipe*, 27/28.12.75.

opposite is true. There is a steady increase in violence in sport, primitive aggression, deliberate brutality, collisions, clashes and conflicts, which at inter-state level reach war-like proportions. Tough tactics are spreading in every field of sport. There are more and more refereeing incidents, vendettas between players, invasions of the field by wild crowds, gratuitous violence on the part of spectators and so on. The wave of violence in sport, totally contradicting the ideology of sportsmanship naïvely peddled by the promoters, is merely the transposition of the violence of the social relations of capitalist production, the rule of every man for himself and the 'struggle for life'.[21] All the values of the capitalist jungle are played out in sport: virility, sexual athleticism, physical dominance, the superman, muscle worship, fascistic male chauvinism, racism, sexism etc. Rugby provides a perfect illustration of the spectacle of violence obligingly displayed year in year out on the T.V. screens. In a society fascinated by murderous exploits it is not surprising to note the *open approval of physical violence* on the part of the press. Rugby is depicted as the ideal preparation for life, an initiative rite for admittance into male society, the source of the body-beautiful that up-and-coming young executives dream of. A good example is provided by the following passage from an article in *Cosmopolitan* devoted to the virile glories of rugby: 'The scrum: the high-point of the game. Two blocks of eight forwards, one and a half tons of "meat", buttressing and pushing each other so as to shove over the others.'[22]

Anyone who knows what really goes on during the course of a rugby, soccer or handball game can appreciate the necessity for sport to develop this fantasy world built around legionnaires, paratroopers, strongmen, cowboys and ladykillers playing imaginary or real roles of avenger, destroyer, or the handsome blond beast giving as good as he gets . . . without troubling his conscience.[23]

21. Cf. R. Cousty, 'Rollerball! Fascination et fascisation des corps', in l'Ecole Emancipée, No. 5, Nov. 1975.
22. 'Vive le foot! (avec lui),' Cosmopolitan, Nov. 1975. This magazine, it should be remembered, is ideologically aimed at young executives and urban petty-bourgeois who consider themselves 'liberated' as far as morality goes.
23. In this respect we strongly recommend G. Falconnet and N. Lefaucheur's remarkable work, La fabrication des mâles, le Seuil, Paris, 1975 (especially the passages devoted to 'male' prejudices in sport and the male chauvinist myths of sportsmen).

In this context of obsession with productivity and success, on this battlefield ruled by the stopwatch, in this symbolic war in which the aim is to conquer both oneself and the opponents, to win at any costs, it is only to be expected that accidents, physical injuries and handicaps and even deaths are increasingly frequent. *Sportsmen literally dice with death.*[24] This is true of motorcycle and car races, cycle racing and climbing expeditions, but it is truer still of skiing competitions. The winter sports circus organises skiing events as a sort of leap into the void, a dive into the absolute and unknown, or as a confrontation with nothingness and with death – the skier's constant companion and permanent risk. The intensity of the competition, the perfection of his equipment – ultra-streamlined suits, cosmonauts' helmets and super-sophisticated skis – the speed of the slopes and the rationalisation of technique turn the skier into a flying comet: a 'snow-borne kamikaze' as a journalist aptly put it.[25] Moreover the safety measures are not always what they should be – after all, profitability comes first! Dr. C. Toubeau, a member of the medical commission of the French ski federation declared in a recent interview: '*A ski team is virtually a hospital.* At a recent congress on traumatology I had the oportunity to draw up an account of all the accidents that had affected the French team. The list was so staggering that everyone laughed . . . There is no doubt that skiers are going ever faster. And though their equipment has improved, that doesn't prevent accidents.'[26] To increase speed, any technological improvement goes, even if it puts the skiers' life in danger. 'As for ski suits', Dr. Toubeau went on, 'they became so smooth in order to cut down wind resistance that the skiers slid a fearful distance when they fell. It took an accident to a German skier during training at Saint-Moritz for such suits to be banned. All this is unacceptable.'[27] This fact has not stopped the fantastic race towards the abyss as the Germans, Swiss, Italians,

24. In an imperialist society which worships death, kills on a grand scale, praises death with shouts of 'viva la muerta', while rushing towards its own destruction.
25. *L'Humanité-Dimanche*, No. 247, 7.12.75.
26. 'The Winter Olympics – the Trade Fair has replaced the Festival', in *Témoignage chrétien*, 12.2.76, p. 13.
27. Ibid. This observation is nothing new. Cf. *Le Monde*, 3.1.74 ('The dangers of skiing'): 'Doctors have proposed that measures be taken to prevent modern textiles "rubbing up" the skier as well as his skis, turning a skier who falls at high speed into a human cannon-ball.'

Austrians and French (not to speak of the Canadians and the rest) develop new 'secret weapons'. Each country is building up its sports arsenal. Laboratory tests are used to discover the techniques and equipment needed to attain crazy speeds. The maximum and average speeds reached in the down-hill events are steadily increasing: 75, 80, 90 m.p.h. At Cervina, in Italy, maximum speeds of up to 125 m.p.h. have been clocked up. So, it should come as no surprise that the list of top-level skiers, seriously injured or killed on the 'field of battle' for a few dollars (or rather medals) more, grows steadily longer.[28]

This absurd, inhuman obsession with winning is not limited to skiing. Present day rugby is a perfect illustration of this fascistic delirium. The masses are expected to mindlessly cheer on a series of pitched battles and wild mauls in which new-style thugs knock each other about. Rugby is a text book case of tolerated violence and the deliberate cultivation of brutality. It reflects the torture mentality and the cult of physical force and confrontation typical of the goon squads of creeping fascism. However, those who sing the praises of this noble sport can no longer conceal the fact that the risks of the game are on the increase and accidents are becoming alarmingly frequent – an awkward fact for a 'game' which is supposed to be 'educative'. Crushing body charges, ruthless tackles, vendettas between players, jarring falls, players trampled under studded boots, the war of the giants of the line out, the clash of heads as the scrum goes down, (the 'battering ram' as the players call it), short arm tackles and the rest, all add to the number of serious injuries and lengthen the list of rugby's victims. Last year a prop forward for a Paris club, G. Magendie died as a result of a spine injury. The French international B. Dauga suffered a period of paralysis after a tackle. The list of often unpublished injuries is steadily growing. The reason for this disturbing recurrence is plain. Larger and larger sums of money are involved. More and more is at stake, whether in international competition where no quarter is given – just look at the South-African muscle machines for instance – or at local level where bitter rivalries come into play, especially in the South of France.

28. The latest being Michel Dujon. Comment of the unfortunate boy's parents: 'You can't stay in mourning for ever. Your job is to carry on, picking up the torch where Michel left off.' (*L'Humanité-Dimanche*, 7.12.75).

Hardly a match goes by without some player being 'taken out' or an outbreak of fist fighting, to the polite disapproval of the connoisseurs. As a journalist recently put it:

'The increasingly rough tactics being used by the players are increasing the risk of accidents. Twenty years ago the clubs were all on the look out for three-quarters. Now they are only interested in props and second-row forwards. Each team is looking for players capable of dominating the field. Last season's wave of accidents indicate a return to tough tactics'[29] – a nice euphemism if ever there was one.

Another characteristic feature of present day competitive sport, which is coming in for criticism even from some fervent advocates of competition, is the total, not to say *totalitarian mobilisation* of the athletes to produce maximum performance. This might even be described as a scientifically superior form of legalised torture.[30] Every sport now involves a fantastic *manipulation of human robots* by doctors, psychologists, bio-chemists and trainers. The 'manufacturing of champions' is no longer a craft but an industry, calling on specialised laboratories, research institutes, training camps and experimental sports centres. Most top-level athletes are reduced to the status of more or less voluntary guinea pigs. 'Hopefuls' are spotted young, the less talented are methodically weeded out and those that remain are then systematically orientated according to their potential. Training attains insane proportions, preparation for the Olympics is organised in Stakhanovite lines, scientific advisers confer at top level to submit every detail of the athletes' lives to medical control: all this brain-

29. M. Labro, 'Is rugby dangerous?', *l'Express*, 16/22.2.76. 'An official doctor of the French rugby federation has worked out that this sport causes twice as many accidents as football, three times as many as skiing and four times as many as basket-ball.' (Ibid.).

30. One might suggest that Amnesty International or the Russell Tribunal carry out an enquiry into sport as a form of torture in countries where the practice of competitive sport is legally compulsory. This form of torture, while not as brutal or crude as the operations of the professional torturers, is nonetheless real and widespread. It has the advantage of being less visible and more subtle since it takes place in a sphere of public life which give the impression of being devoid of all bodily constraint, enslavement or humiliation. However sport is perhaps the social practice which best exemplifies the 'disciplinary society', analysed by M. Foucault in *Discipline and Punish*, Penguin Hardback, London 1978 (see also our text: *Corps et Politique*, op. cit.).

washing and Pavlovian conditioning goes into producing the necessary quantity of top-class thoroughbreds, ready to hold their own in the competitive madhouse. The specialists in this sporting Gulag stop at no human sacrifice in their drive to push back the limits of human capacity and transcend biological barriers. Whatever the well-intentioned acolytes of the sports institution may say, everyday, body-fascism is alive and well in this scientific production of the 'élite of the human race' . . . And these are the methods that our rulers and educationalists wish to generalise, for the sake of improving the sports results of the nation!

In case anyone thinks this is an exaggeration, it is worth merely recalling some current practices in this field. In a recent article published by *Reader's Digest*, Ron Clarke, former 5,000 and 10,000 metres record holder, who can thus be considered an 'effort specialist', revealed, or rather recalled the techniques and technological discoveries used to bring about considerable organic mutations, changes in the structure of muscular and cardio-vascular output, physiological equilibrium, brain functioning etc. This was how *l'Equipe* reported the criticisms raised by the former slave of the track:

'In many countries computers have for several years now been used to calculate the breaking points of the human body and decide just how much training a given individual can stand. The same computers can infallibly pick out the young people who have the best chance of being the champions of the future. To get clear answers all you have to do is feed the machine with data on the psychological make-up, the character and the life-style of the subject. Ron Clarke also condemns countries which attempt to indoctrinate children from an early age, sometimes from as early as 3 or 4 years old, using a sort of brain-washing technique to instil them with a special type of culture so that sport for them becomes an organic habit — a second nature — on which their lives are mentally and physically dependent. Clarke then has a go at the scientists who carry out the practice of taking a certain quantity of blood from an individual and then trans-fusing it back again, which has the effect of extending the limits of endurance by raising the level of haemoglobin retention. Similarly, athletes are put on a special dietary regime[31] in which

31. Expression, which, given its political connotation, is particularly sinister in this context . . .

three days without carbohydrates are alternated with three days of absorbtion of large doses of carbohydrates, giving rise to weight gains of the order of three pounds. Clarke's charge sheet also takes in the artificial building of muscle tissue using electrodes and the abuse of synthetic hormones by both men and women. Other no less current practices are reviewed.'[32]

E. Germany, which has become the universal example for all countries seeking to turn themselves into sport factories, has raised the Gulag-like organisation of biological and psychological manipulation to the level of a state institution. This is why for some time now the most moderate of observers have been posing serious questions about the treatment accorded to their athletes. Recent revelations (which are sometimes motivated by anti-communist propaganda) have brought to light the reality of the process of production of champions in this, the world's leading sporting nation. In a recent article devoted to 'the manufacturing of swimmers in E. Germany', F. Janin gave a well confirmed account of some of the special medical conditioning techniques employed in the training camps, which some people go so far as to describe as detention centres.

'The E. German doctors', he wrote, 'are said to have developed undetectable drugs. These are widely used for scientific purposes. So as not to have an adverse effect on the athlete's self-confidence, this medical doping is carried out without his knowledge, except in the case of "safe elements" and adults. Roland Matthes is said to be in this category and all the new doping techniques have been tried out on him. Matthes, the four times Olympic champion, is said to be the chief guinea pig. Treatment with anabolic steroids has been generalised, together with the introduction of male hormones for girls, even the very young. In support of these reports, it is worrying to note the metamorphosis of the young E. German girl swimmers over the years. Once slim, slightly built and feminine, they soon become thick set and undergo deformations which indeed seem suspect. One of the main preoccupations of these new sorcerers has been to roll back

32. R. Parienté, 'Un procureur nommé Ron Clarke,' l'Equipe, 27/28.12.75. Parienté adds the comment: 'This study leaves you with a nasty taste in your mouth. Is that really what sport is all about?' If the question is posed, the answer can only be yes – there is only one kind of sport – the kind you can see with your own two eyes!

the fatigue barrier. Each swimmer's sporting activity is monitored
by computer. Every swimmer has his punch card.[33] On the basis
of this information and permanent medical surveillance, it is said
to be possible to determine the fatigue barrier, and hence the
theoretical limitations of each subject, with an accuracy of 98%.
That's when the injection of toxins, a sort of anti-fatigue vaccine,
comes in. All these practices, using steroids and various kinds of
injections are freely tried out in swimming . . . Laboratories are
at the disposal of the three chief trainers, the fifty ordinary
trainers and the one hundred and twenty doctors responsible for
the development of swimming in E. Germany. This is also said
to be why no Westerner has ever been allowed into one of the
special training camps.'[34]

Today doping scandals are springing up like mushrooms. No
sport is unaffected, whether it be athletics, cycling, cross-country
skiing or rowing. At the Innsbruck Winter Olympics there was a
series of disciplinary measures for drug abuse. The Soviet cross-
country ski champion, Galina Kulakova, was disqualified for having
taken a drug containing a banned substance, ephedrine. The
Czech ice-hockey team was disciplined for doping, when one of the
team members was found guilty of taking codeine, a powerful
pain-killer banned by the medical commission of the International
Olympic Committee; and the Czech team doctor was banned for
life from the Olympic movement. Worse still, also at the Innsbruck
Olympics, the Norwegian team officially notified the IOC medical
commission of the practice of doping by means of blood transfusions. This practice was said to be widely used by certain
countries, in particular E. Germany (once again), to benefit their
cross-country skiers and was already in regular use by Finnish and
New Zealand athletes as well as by racing cyclists the world over.

33. Keeping files on sportsmen and citizens in general seems to be all the
    rage just about everywhere in the world, not just in the 'advanced
    liberal régime' of Giscard, Chirac and Poniatowski . . .
34. Le Monde, 9/10.9.73. F. Janin adds the following remark: 'The E.
    German teams are not just accompanied, they are guarded and kept
    under close watch. Every step an athlete or a swimmer takes is pre-
    planned and it is impossible to meet them unless they are accompanied
    by a 'body guard', or even two. When, after persistent requests, a press
    conference is eventually organised, the answers to all the questions are
    the same: 'Everything is fine. Everyone is happy. We have no training
    secrets. We like music.'

This rather special technique operates by stimulating the body's corpuscle regulation process.

A quantity of blood is removed shortly before a particularly demanding competition. This creates a shortage which is compensated for by the production of red corpuscles. The blood is then re-transfused into the same person, giving rise to a surplus of red corpuscles which is held to 'improve oxygenation and pep up the athlete, thereby improving his performance. By using this artificial procedure sportsmen are in fact attempting to reproduce the surplus of red corpuscles which results from adaptation to high altitudes, and which enables an athlete competing shortly afterwards at sea level to improve his results.'[35] Faced with the spread of this sort of practice[36] which 'treat the athletes as so many guinea pigs',[37] most sports and medical authorities feel obliged to react. The IOC has just launched an official campaign, warning of the danger to the athletes' health represented by such goings on. Similarly, the president of the European Athletics Association has declared his firm intention to take action against doping. As R. Pointu has stressed in this regard:

'It's now an open secret: the constant rise in the level of performance has turned some athletes into sorcerer's apprentices. Doctors are as yet unable to gauge the seriousness of the threat to health posed by anabolic steroids taken so as to stay in the race after medals and records.'[38]

Thus in the fight against the scourge of doping, which as cycling has shown, can easily give rise to serious and even fatal accidents, the sports authorities are introducing more and more preventive measures, threats, surveillance of athletes, blood tests, urine tests,

35. *Le Monde*. 7.2.76.
36. Now, in the case of cyclists for example, they are even resorting to complete blood transfusions 'with the aim of ridding the blood of the toxins built up by sustained effort. This flies in the face of the fact that these toxins are warning signals and to ignore them means putting the heart in danger'. (ibid.). It should be noted in passing that however scandalous these blood transfusion methods may seem, they merely reflect the capitalist and imperialist blood market: (class inequalities for transfusions, the international blood traffic organised by the monopolies, the removal of blood on an industrial scale from poor and oppressed so-called 'volunteers', ideological speculation surrounding bood donation and so on).
37. *Le Monde*, 15/16.2.76.
38. 'La chasse aux anabolisants', *Le Monde*, 24.2.76.

new techniques for detecting banned substances and of course disciplinary measures. In other words, within the institution of sport, generally described as educative, liberating and fulfilling, we see the outbreak of the same contradictions to be found in the police-style regimentation of hearts and minds in capitalist society in general – a society haunted by the totalitarian dream of absolute control over people's private lives. The sports and medical authorities, reigning hand in hand over a system governed by the logic of competition and productivity, inevitably give birth to a strengthened judicial and police apparatus. 'Do we have to face more and more supervision, all year round, both of the competitions themselves and of training? That would mean turning the world of athletics (and of all other sports events) into a huge police operations area, and would seriously infringe on the athletes' private life.'[39]

To give some idea of the alienation involved in sport, stemming from the oppression of the body pushed to the limits of physical effort, mention still has to be made of the repression which the athletes voluntarily undergo in the course of competition or training. Suffering in sport has today reached truly inhuman proportions. Contemporary ideologists hold up the 'pleasures of sport'[40] as an example for young people. But in reality, at the present day level of competition, sport means tearing your guts out, writhing in pain, and sweating it out all day long in the toil and torment of physical effort for its own sake. *The sporting legend is above all else a story of the pain barrier, of going to the limits of endurance, of being drunk with 'animal' fatigue and of getting a kick out of bruises, knocks and injuries.* The intensive practice of sport is an institutionalised celebration of the mortification of the flesh, the acting out of a sado-masochistic ideology. Its compulsive repetitiveness and sexual frustration are sure signs of the neurotic obsession of the ascetic with discipline and self-mastery. As C. Montaignac wrote in *l'Equipe:*

39. Ibid.
40. Jean Prévost, *Plaisirs des sports, essais sur le corps humain,* Gallimard, Paris 1925, which has become a classic on sports ethics. Cf. p. 22: 'Thus first of all I experienced the pleasure of performance. Then as soon as I had obtained the first results I became increasingly meticulous and careful, concentrating on perfection. I had acquired the puritanical spirit, the sense of devotion and the need of duty which inspire such regulated and consecrated, prayer-like gestures.'

'Down through the centuries sport has been the refuge of sublimated pain. From the soldier at Marathon to the victor of a mountain section in the Tour de France and the oarsmen collapsing in agony, men have always sung of the hero's exhaustion.'[41]

At the level of social imagination, sport's paths of suffering[42] constitute a real mystique of the outstanding individual devoting himself body and soul to the accomplishment of his 'physical duty', demanding total self-denial and going as far as the 'supreme sacrifice' – death. Then at the level of the individual athlete's fantasies about his own body, the regular dose of suffering becomes an indispensable *drug*. These modern apostles of corporal repression like nothing better than to wallow in quasi-religious experiences colourfully described as getting your face re-arranged, flogging yourself to death, sinking into the mists of suffocation, relishing the joys of muscular exhaustion or bursting your heart out! Montaignac, pursuing his hymn to the heroes of effort, had this to say following an enquiry into physical and mental pain in top-level competition: 'This "body count" shows that the fight against oneself carried to the limits of endurance produces sensations which are experienced only by sportsmen, not to mention masochists.'[43] Too true! Judge for yourselves:

– *Michel Jazy*: It starts to hurt deep in your throat. The blood rushes up. You feel sick, your stomach muscles knot up and your legs feel like lead.

– *Alain Mimoun*: In the marathon there is always a terrible moment of weakness. In my case, at Melbourne, everything went all right up to the 32nd. kilometre, then a sudden weakness. I felt as if I was only advancing a few inches with every stride. I started talking to myself, telling myself to react and even swearing at myself. That's when you are up against yourself. I couldn't take it – my blood just stopped circulating.

– *J-P. Jarrier* (racing driver): In the car it's sheer hell. You get the feeling your body's gone haywire, but you keep going to the end. The incentive of a Grand Prix helps us to stand the pain.

41. *L'Equipe*, 26.2.76.
42. Ibid.
43. Ibid.

– *Yves Fraysse* (oarsman): Up to the middle of the race the fatigue increases. You're practically dead, but you have to carry on. To reduce the pain you think about how much the others are suffering. Your thighs swell up, your arms hardly make it and your back stops responding. When you get to 1,500 metres, you tell yourself that if you had any sense you'd stop there and then. But you have to keep going. Right up to the end the burning sensation gets worse – you feel as if your whole body is on fire from head to toe . . . rowing involves 100% effort and that means 100% pain.

– *B. Thevenet* (cyclist): The feeling of lack of air is terrible. You think you're going to pass out – that you're not far from dying. It's true, you say to yourself maybe that's what dying feels like.

– *P. Trentin* (cyclist): Your thigh muscles swell up as if you were going to burst. You zig-zag along. The whole body is under terrible pressure. You're like a galley slave.

– *Carlos Bianchi* (footballer): The knocks you get really hurt . . . But you have to stay in the match, go into a tackle, take the knocks and carry on as hard as ever.

– *P. Gourrier* (weight lifter): In training: that's where you get the worst fatigue. A long session lasts three or four hours. If you total up all the weights it comes to 20 tons. Amongst ourselves we admit to being completely shattered. We really hit rock bottom.

– *J-P. Coche* (judo): You can't pin down exactly where you feel the pain. It hurts all over . . . Sometimes it's all you can do not to fall. You have to get past terrible moments of emptiness . . . Once I could no longer hear anything. I carried on the match like an automaton.

– *A. Boulouche* (wrestler): If you can keep going the pain is terrible. You have to understand that in wrestling we are often injured – little injuries, such as finger injuries for example, which are nonetheless very painful. To stand up to certain holds with this sort of injury is a hard trial. But exhaustion also results from mental suffering.

– *R. Quémener* (walker): The pain gets worse as you approach 200 kilometres. You have to concentrate to be able to stand it. You talk as little as possible. Fatigue sets in first of course in your legs and hip joints. But worst is the treatment your feet get . . . It takes a sort of madness to keep us going. On our own we couldn't do it. But thanks to the people round about we manage to stand up to the pain. Maybe you have to be a bit of a masochist to go through this pain. And there is an element of sadism in the public's response . . . People don't come to see great walkers. They come to see men suffering.

– *P. Moreau* (swimmer): Your stomach tightens and your guts knot up. You feel as if you had a blow torch under your stomach. Your body goes rigid, especially around the arms.

– *Walter Spangerro* (rugby): You have to go beyond suffering. The bruises come out after the match, but the pain is bearable. At the end of a match I have sometimes not even had the strength to get undressed. There are times when will-power enables us to do things which the body can't take. Mentally you are prepared, but not physically. That's when it's hard – you are smashed. It's true that the knocks wear you out, there's no question.[44]

We have quoted at length from this anthology of 'sporting culture' because it is a perfect illustration of the reactionary ideological functions of sport, especially at the level of mass psychology:

(a) Sport is a very prevalent form of 'practical reason' (in the Kantian sense), which contains all the values of traditional, repressive morality and hence all the models of behaviour promoted by bourgeois society: the cult of duty for its own sake, the sense of sacrifice for the community, the ideology of the super-ego, obedience, discipline etc . . .[45] Take for example what the sports advocate, P. Morand, has to say: 'There is nothing magic about the virtues of the winner. They are the same as those found in every kind of exemplary life: concentration, method, organisation, persistence and will-power, *independent of the slightest pleasure.*' (Quoted in *l'Equipe*, 5.1.76.) In other words, the champions' virtues are those of the ideal Mr. Average, well-adjusted, respectful of the established order, a tireless worker, a citizen above

44. Ibid.
45. A good illustration of the collaboration between Judeo-Christian morality and 'sports ethics' is given by Y. Brossard's book, *Vues chrétiennes sur le sport*, Flammarion, Paris, 1961.

suspicion, in short, the ideal held up by every handbook of morality and citizenship (and indeed by every Kantian moralist).

(b) As a *libidinal substitute* and a sublimation of agressivity, sport offers its practitioners the possibility to explore their physical being organ by organ, muscle by muscle, limb by limb by gradually experiencing longed for tortures through a *controlled process of self-inflicted punishment* or even self-destruction. In this respect sport is an *institutional neurosis* providing an outlet for 'moral masochism'[46] or in general for what Reich called the 'masochistic character'. This appears to be an element of the mass psychology of the depressed and alienated working population who seek refuge in a *mortified form of sexual pleasure* – a transfiguration or sublimation of death. The institution of sport is thus an outlet for the instinctual drives deriving from *a schizophrenic relationship to the body*. This relationship reflects anxiety in face of erotic pleasure, sensuality and the uncontrollable nature of desire. 'Get your pleasure from pain'[47] has become the slogan of the battalions of suffering paraded on the sports grounds and in the swimming pools.

(c) Sport represents a veritable *ideological apparatus of death*. Physical torture, tolerated and put on as entertainment, is held up as politically neutral and culturally legitimate. Sport gets the masses used to wildly applauding the exploits of men and women submitting their bodies to a refined, superior form of internalised and accepted suffering. This set up has two kinds of beneficial effects for the defence of the established order. On the one hand it legitimises all the current forms of torture and ill-treatment by exorcising them on 'another stage' – on the sports field (which, by the way, is often the scene of acts of physical terror and torture, as in the Santiago stadium after the Coup d'Etat in Chile). It conditions people to accept as 'natural' all the aggressions, injuries, mutilations and physical suffering so liberally dispensed by

46. Cf. S. Nacht, *le Masochisme*, Petite bibliothèque Payot, Paris, 1965, p. 5: 'Masochism is a neuro-pathological state characterised by the seeking of pain. The masochist experiences a real need or thirst for pain. This pain may be physical or mental, or both at once.' Cf. also articles by F. Gantheret and G. Berthaud in *Partisans, sport, culture et répression*, op. cit.

47. S. Freud, *Papers on Metapsychology* in The Standard Edition of the complete psychological work of S. Freud, Vol 14, The Hogarth Press, London 1957.

most contemporary governments. The sports crowd's yells of 'Take him out!' correspond to the police slogan 'Have a go!' On the other hand, the spectacle of sport operates as a political economy of licit cruelty which enables, to the advantage of the ruling classes, a fantastic diversion of the aggresion of the masses resulting from all the frustrations, disillusions and disappointments engendered by capitalism. Thus the masses' capacity for revolt and struggle, instead of being directed against the 'cruel masters' who oppress, repress and culturally impoverish them, is transformed into *organic self-reppression*.

By conforming their body to the severe prescriptions of their masters, the slaves come to forget their condition as slaves and ignore the social conditions responsible for their slavery.[48] The lavish spectacle of sportsmen's bodies so generously sacrificed makes it possible to *numb* people's feelings to the groans, suffering and torture of hundreds and thousands of political prisoners all over the world and the everyday physical violence perpetrated against millions of outcasts interned in the ghettoes of our time. Just look at South Africa for example, where sport reigns supreme.[49]

Another aspect of sporting alienation becoming more and more visible concerns the complete mechanisation of sportsmen. They are integrated into a mechanical system and their bodies are machined by human engineers and body technocrats. In general, sport might be regarded as a sort of mega-machine within which performance-machines, a superior form of automaton as it were, operate in a symbolic world of figures, computers, curves, stopwatch times and quantified energy. 'There are machines everywhere, in the literal sense of the term: machines for producing other machines with their couplings and interconnexions,' wrote G. Deleuze and F. Guattari.[50] Their's is an accurate description of the sports system with its modern industrialised mechanisms, its feed-back processes and its complex,

48. Cf. J.-M. Brohm, 'Psychanalyse et révolution', in *Partisans*: *Gardefous arrêtez de vous serrer les coudes*, Petite collection Maspéro, Paris, 1975.
49. Cf. *Droit et liberté* ('Non au racisme dans le sport'), monthly review of the movement against racism and anti-semitism and for peace (MRAP), No. 334, Nov. 1974.
50. G. Deleuze and F. Guattari, *l'Anti Œdipe*, Editions de Minuit, Paris, 1972, p. 7.

bureaucratised network of interactions. The ideal situation for sport is for the system to be reliable, computerised, operating without hitches or incidents according to a pre-established programme and in function of pre-ordained objectives. Sport embodies the totalitarian dream of a system run on completely cybernetic lines, developing sporting 'cybernetropes', to borrow H. Lefebvre's expression, destined to serve as 'guides for the human race'.[51]

It is clear that *the vocabulary of the machine dominates the language of sport*. The body is reduced to the status of a machine or a quantity of energy. Terms such as 'human motor' and 'animal machine' are in current use. Reference is made to energy output and the efficiency of muscle sections. The slang employed by sportsmen is often drawn from the workings of a machine: 'He's revving up'; 'She's burning up the track'; 'He's working well – turning out results – producing the goods . . .' When athletes break down their machine 'seizes up' or 'runs out of steam!' When the race is comfortable, the runner becomes 'a well-oiled machine' which 'eats up the kilometres!' His 'engine races', or 'passes into overdrive'. In short the semantic tools are predominantly drawn from technology, clearly indicating that sport treats the body as an engine, as a specially equipped apparatus, as an instrument and in fact as a reified ballistic object in abstract space-time. The language of mechanics is chosen as the most appropriate to describe the workings of a mechanically objectified body. Team work in sport is thus regarded as a collective mechanical operation. For example, P. Morand, referring to a relay team, speaks of *'the joint effort forging them into a single eight-rod engine block.'*[52]

Adorno and Horkheimer have observed that, 'The oarsmen, who cannot speak to one another, are each of them yoked in the same rhythm as the modern worker in a factory . . .'[53]

This notion of a great machine or collective block has made its way into the consciousness of today's sportsmen. Describing the

51. In the somewhat disturbing words of a CP ideologist. Cf. 'Le parti communiste français et les activités sportives et physiques', in *l'Ecole et la Nation*, No. 180, June 1969, p. 47.
52. P. Morand, *World Champions*, William Heinemann, 1931, p. 6 (Ian Fraser's translation has been kept here—Ed.).
53. T. W. Adorno and M. Horkheimer, *Dialectic of Enlightenment*, Allan Lane, London, 1971.

activity of the E. German hand-ball team, M. Castaing wrote:

'That's the most striking feature of the E. German representatives, which could well cause problems for human harmony: the impression of quiet power and imperturbable calm given by this team. *Every cog appears to fit in perfectly with the others, Rarely can the comparison of a sports team with a machine have been more accurate: the E. German team is like a steam-roller made up of tireless human robots* capable of keeping up the same pace for an hour, physically and mentally cast in the same mould: cast-iron morale, steely nerves and brazen muscles. *It would almost be true to speak of a team of steel-makers.'*[54]

1976 is another Olympic year. The ideological mystification of sport is sure to intensify. That is why international revolutionaries have the task of developing a campaign condemning the Olympic publicity circus and the police saturation that are being prepared for Montreal, on the same lines as at Innsbruck. At the time of the Munich Games in 1972, the French revolutionary organisations launched a united anti-Olympic committee. One of the committee's press statements declared: [55]

'The nations represented at the Munich Olympics are joining in chorus to try to convince the peoples of the world of the reality of a general truce in the political conflicts between nations, "races" and classes in the name of "universal brotherhood". The undersigned organisations condemn the Olympics as a mystification aiming to have us forget the daily reality of imperialist aggression against oppressed people and the capitalist exploitation and oppression of the workers.

'We condemn the fine speeches in favour of peace made by the representatives of all the countries present at the Games, at the very time when the dykes in North Vietnam are being systematically bombed by American imperialism.

'We condemn the idea of a truce in the class struggle, while man-hunts, generalised torture and states of emergency are normal practice in a series of military dictatorships both on the

54. *Le Monde*, 7.3.70.
55. Cf. The special issue of *Le Chrono Enrayé* ('bilan des J. O. de Munich'), supplement to the review *Ecole Emancipée*, No. 2, 30.9.72. On the challenge to the Munich Games, see also the remarkable pamphlet, *Munich 1972, la 'paix olympique', prélude à notre apocalypse quotidienne, Commune libre*, No. 1, Toulouse, Dec. 1972.

American continent (where 16 Argentinian revolutionaries have just been cold-bloodedly murdered) and in Africa and western Europe (Greece, Spain, Portugal, Northern Ireland).

'We condemn the complicity of the Stalinist régimes with this mystification in the name of peaceful coexistence. Through this complicity they themselves seek to hide their own crimes (the Prague trials, the repression of workers' struggles in Poland, internment in psychiatric hospitals).

'We stress that the mystification operated through the Olympics is just the most flagrant expression of the regimentation of the masses and especially of young people by means of competitive sport, which has become a true opiate of the people.

'We call on all our members in their fields of intervention, and more generally, on all those who stand for the ideas of May '68 to develop and intensify anti-Olympic propaganda.

'The initial signatories call on other organisations which have not yet become involved to associate themselves with this appeal.'

(A.M.R. – Ecole Emancipée – Gauche Marxiste – Ligue Communiste – Révolution! – 1.9.72.)

Today the combined crisis of imperialism and Stalinism makes such a campaign even more significant. 1976 will undoubtedly be the year of reckoning for sport, the more so for the fact that most of the critical analyses made of the institution are being confirmed in practice. The recent Innsbruck Olympics and the 'catastrophic' state of preparation of the Montreal Games have shown the extent to which capitalist involvement in sport has become an affair of state, giving rise to a fierce battle between rival interests,[56] trusts and multinational companies. They show the size of the publicity and commercial interests tied to the Olympic circus

56. To take only one example: at the Innsbruck Olympics, the imperialist firm Honeywell Bull, through its Austrian subsidiary, landed the tender offered by the Games organisation committee for the instantaneous processing and broadcasting of results. The contract was worth 1.75 m francs. Every result flashed on television was thus accompanied by the firm's name, providing several hours of free, officially permitted advertising. As *Le Monde* wrote (15.1.76): 'Grenoble 1968 . . . Sapporo 1972 . . . Innsbruck 1976. The Olympics come and go and one is much like another. The five rings of the Olympic symbol are still a good selling point and a good number of manufacturers are just as keen to get the right to the label 'official suppliers to the Olympic games'.

and the importance of the Games for the national economy of the organising country.[57]

Above all, the current Olympic year proves to those who may have forgotten, that the 'Games of friendship, peace and brotherhood' essentially represent a huge preventive police operation, involving the total militarisation of the Olympic area. Since the events at Munich, the obsession with security and public order is such that the Games have become the pretext for Ministries of the Interior to organise dress rehearsals for eventual operations to deal with 'trouble-makers' and to carry out preventive measures to deal with the 'terrorists'. At Innsbruck the Olympic village was like a fortified camp, occupied by the various security forces. As Le Monde reported (5.2.76):

'The security measures for Innsbruck are impressive. Two thousand five hundred security officers, including policemen, soldiers and even specially recruited private detectives are on duty. There are five policemen for every athlete ... The Olympic village has been turned into a real stronghold. It is surrounded by a high fence fitted with alarm systems and lit up all night long by powerful searchlights. The entrance is guarded round the clock and no one can get past without all the necessary passes. An electronic detection system, similar to those used at airports, enables the guards to detect the presence of any arms. If, for example, a journalist wishes to meet an athlete, he is accompanied by a police officer right up to the café of the athletics section. There, a hostess goes to find the sportsman he wishes to see. All personalities are permanently protected by the state police. Their official cars will be driven by security agents. This huge array of security forces is completed by an anti-terrorist squad, an arsenal of various kinds of arms, a hundred radio cars and several helicopters. And finally, as the Olympics approach, special checks are being carried out at the Austrian frontier.'[58]

It is hardly surprising that in this world of cops, strong-arm men and bodyguards a psychosis concerning terrorism has de-

57. On this question, Cf. the special issue of Quel Corps?, No. 4/5, April 1976, devoted to the Montreal Olympics.
58. So as not to be left behind in this security race, Canada has just taken a series of measures with the purpose of being able to prevent persons suspected of 'terrorist activities' from crossing her borders. (Cf. L'Equipe, 4.3.76).

veloped, leading to an obsession with security and calls for informers. The police have already carried out several inquiries into 'suspicious situations', false alarms and anonymous telephone calls.

A fruitless search of the Seefeld region, 25 kilometres from Innsbruck, where the cross-country events were due to take place, was carried out after the presence of members of the Baader-Meinhof group had been reported in the area. (*le Monde* 14.2.76.) The General Secretary of the Innsbruck Games organisation committee confirmed the existence of international cooperation between the police forces of the Common Market. 'Our police are cooperating closely with the police forces of our neighbouring countries. The frontiers are being kept under watch and reports are being drawn up on the movements of all suspicious groups in the direction of Austria.' (*l'Equipe*, 26.1.76.) The Austrian weekly *Profil* estimated the total budget for security at 30 million schillings. What a wonderful picture of the smiling democratic face of the Olympic movement! But then of course in Austria and Germany there is a certain tradition of camps, particularly the kind that are protected by searchlights and watchtowers, police-dogs and fences of every kind. A top Austrian police official, showing considerable candour, confided to *Profil* the concentration camp philosophy behind the strong-arm state: 'The best possible form of security measure requires a visible presence. The peaceful image of the Games is bound to take a bit of a knock. Policemen wearing steel helmets and carrying light machine guns will be *a normal part of the street scene* during the Games.' (*l'Equipe* 23.1.76.)

The troops and security forces are already on the alert for the Montreal Games. Most of the force, consisting of 10,000 men, will be furnished by the Canadian armed forces and reserve units. To this number will be added various police forces, special security agents, the gentlemen of the CIA and the FBI, the strong-arm men of every nationality and so on. We are well on the way to replacing the Olympic meeting with a cops' jamboree!

Because, as *Libération* put it (10.12.75), sport is 'an ideal instrument for manipulating minds and bodies', whether by capitalism in the West or by bureaucratic state capitalism in the East, it is quite illusory to think it can be reformed or prettified by a purge or by removing certain abuses and deformities. It is just as naïve to try to rid sport of its negative aspects as to try and democratise

34

the bourgeois or Stalinist state. Some people dream of a healthy, educative kind of sport, based nonetheless on the same principles as at present – competition, training, maximum output, selection, spectacle etc. Marx's reply to Bray is extremely apt in relation to these ideas:

'Mr Bray turns the *"illusion"* of the respectable bourgeois into an *ideal* he would like to attain. In a purified individual exchange, freed from all the elements of antagonism he finds in it, he sees an *equalitarian* relation which he would like society to adopt. Mr Bray does not see that this *equalitarian* relation, this *corrective ideal* that he would like to apply to the world, is itself nothing but the reflection of the actual world; and that therefore it is totally impossible to reconstitute society on the basis of what is merely an embellished shadow of it. In proportion as this shadow takes on substance again, we perceive that this substance, far from being the transfiguration dreamt of, is the actual body of existing society.'[59]

Our task is to smash this 'present day body of society' (and in particular its back-bone – the bourgeois state apparatus), and the form of bodily activity dominating capitalist society – the competitive relationship – in order to build a communist society and develop a non-alienated culture of the body.

Jean-Marie BROHM
Paris, March 1976.

59. K. Marx, *The Poverty of Philosophy*, in K. Marx/F. Engels, *Collected Works*, Vol. 6, Lawrence & Wishart, London, 1975, p. 144.

THE SOURCES OF THE TEXTS

– *Sport, culture and repression* is a slightly modified version of the editorial of No. 68 of *Partisans*, 'Sport, culture et répression' (July/September 1968, Maspéro).

– *Theses towards a political sociology of sport*, is an improved version of an article in *Le Chrono Enrayé*, No. 8, May/June 1972.

– *Sport, an ideological state apparatus: the neutrality of the sports-field*, is a reorganised version of an article in *Politique Aujourd'hui* ('idéologie et production culturelle'), October/December 1974.

– *Why the 'Ecole Emancipée' is against competitive sport*, is an extension of an article in *l'Ecole Emancipée*, No. 15, May 1974.

–*The sports mode of production: E. Germany*, was hitherto unpublished.

– *The significance of leisure in the 'leisure civilisation'*, was first published in *Partisans*, Sport, culture et répression, op. cit.

– *The Olympic Opiate*, is a slightly altered version of an article in *Politique Hebdo*, 7.9.72.

– *The Olympic games and the imperialist accumulation of capital*, is the extension of an article in *Le Chrono Enrayé*, No. 8, op. cit.

– *Towards an institutional analysis of competitive sport*, was first published in *l'Homme et la societé* ('analyse institutionnelle et socioanalyse') Nos. 29/30, Anthropos, July/December 1973.

– *The anti-Olympic appeal of the 'Ecole Emancipée'*, was first published in *Le Chrono Enrayé*, No. 9, October/November 1972.

– *The draft appeal for the setting up of an anti-Olympic committee* was first published in *Quel Corps?*, No. 3, November/December 1975.

– *Twenty theses on sport* was first published in *Quel Corps?*, No. 1, April/May, 1975.

– *Appeal for the Boycott of Argentina as Organiser of the Football World Cup* was first published in France in January 1978 by the Collective organising this boycott.

Sport, Culture and Repression*

Sooner or later somebody had to get around to publishing *a critical, revolutionary study of sport, of physical leisure activities and the culture of the body under capitalism*. The revolutionary May events gave me both the possibility and the opportunity to do so, for two reasons.

Firstly, it became strikingly clear that all layers and sectors of bourgeois culture, even those fetishistically considered to be sheltered from the repressive power of the state, are institutionally tied to state structures and in fact constitute appendages of the state. Since the form of bourgeois society in a given period is summed up in its state, it follows, as Marx says in *The German Ideology*, that 'all common institutions are set up with the help of the state and are given a political form'.[1]

This was brought out in a perfectly exemplary way by the May revolution, when all the struggles, even on the artistic and cultural fronts, were objectively directed against *the bourgeois state* which they quickly came up against. In other words, the whole of bourgeois culture, even its most secondary forms, turned out to be essentially repressive. Thus the May revolution enabled us to talk concretely about cultural repression. By denouncing the education system, violently condemning bourgeois culture and shattering bourgeois morality the revolutionary youth created the possibility of a critique of all those forms of repression which are camouflaged under 'democratic' outward appearances in the University, the theatres, the swimming pools and stadiums, in the

*This article is the slightly modified version of the editorial to *Partisans*, No. 68, 'Sport, Culture et répression' (July-September 1968, Maspéro).
1. K. Marx & F. Engels, *The German Ideology*, in K. Marx/F. Engels *Collected Works*, Vol. 5, Lawrence & Wishart, London, 1975, p. 90.

schools, at 'left-wing' festivals and in all other fields of culture. *The lessons of the May events thus challenged us to track down repression wherever it is to be found.*

Then secondly, the revolutionary explosion was above all an explosion of *youth*. 'Run, comrade – the old world is on your heels!': this denunciation of the sclerosis of the bourgeois world matched the celebration of youthfulness expressed in the slogan: 'To be young is an eternal intoxication!' What was in question was the cultural and social fate of young people, down-graded by the Gaullist state and condemned to unemployment, repression and regimentation. The revolutionary youth declared their rights to life, to freedom and to sensual pleasure. 'Let us live'; 'Take your desires for realities!'; 'No obstacles to sensual pleasure!'; 'Live life to the full!'; 'With Marcuse for a new, eroticised society!' – these wall slogans showed a revolutionary will to link demands for the free expression of instinctual drives to political demands, and they are clear proof of the *revolutionary value of Eros in politics*. In this respect, the May revolution was in the tradition of all great revolutionary movements. As Engels stresses, 'It is a curious fact that with every revolutionary movement the question of "free love" comes in to the foreground. With one set of people as a revolutionary progress, as a shaking off of old traditional fetters, no longer necessary . . .'[2] On this front, young people truly carried the torch of the proletarian revolution, both as a vanguard and as a prophetic 'symbol' of the freeing of instinctual drives.

This raises the whole question of the physical life of young people, which is of such concern to sociologists and educationalists. 'Practice sport,' has become a slogan proposed both by the bourgeoisie and by leisure organisations as an answer to the problems of young people. But the revolutionary struggles of young workers and university and school students put into question in a sharper way than ever before the *content of class culture* and the content of the leisure activities and distractions offered to young people. These struggles demonstrated the deeply political side of their demands for the satisfaction of instinctual drives and physical needs, of the 'life-instinct', or the 'instinct for non-sublimated freedom', as Marcuse so well expressed it. Youth's challenge to a repressive culture is also a challenge to the place given to the body

2. F. Engels, *The Book of Revelations*, in F. Marx/F. Engels *On Religion*, Lawrence & Wishart, London, 1957, p. 205.

in the present system. These struggles challenged the values which petrify, enslave, mutilate and repress the body: work, productivity, aggression, heroism, etc.

Young people superbly expressed their determination to submit no longer to the traditional forms of cultural control, refusing the well intentioned paternalism of bourgeois youth organisations. In this respect they were merely extending their struggle against state repression. 'Down with repression!' was their slogan. Through the style of their interventions, through their demands, their sustained and brave struggle, their high level of consciousness and their radical critique, they brought out *the repressive character of all the youth organisations and other institutions* by means of which their activities were controlled – and they went on to smash, momentarily, some of these institutions.

But paradoxically they did not directly attack one of the most repressive structures of bourgeois society – sport and its by-products. (Even in the Charlety Stadium, when a favourable opportunity arose which cried out for the question to be taken up.) *Sport was notable for its absence from the May events.* The revolution passed sport by and so to speak gave it a temporary reprieve. Was this due to indifference? To a great extent, yes. Young people were not interested in sport, despite assertions to the contrary by leaders of the PCF* and its daily paper *l'Humanité,* who were more concerned with the claims of 'sports workers' than with the blows being taken by the leftist students. Young people did not care one bit about sport, much to the despair of their sports teachers, who would have preferred to see them devote more attention to it and less to politics and sex. The contempt in which young people held sport showed that they considered it a pasttime for boy-scouts, right outside their range of interests.

Could the neglect of the question of sport have been due to a lack of information? That too was one of the reasons. The essentially repressive nature of sport was not as immediately obvious as that of the CRS. Moreover, sport was not directly at stake in the struggle. But while sport and repressive physical leisure activities were not present in the consciousness of the protagonists, they were nonetheless indirectly a target of the revolutionary struggle. In taking on the Gaullist state, the young workers and college and school students were at the same time taking on the

*Parti Communiste Français, French Communist Party.

education apparatus which had the job of developing a policy of repression against them. In fighting the structures of that state, they were involved in a head-on struggle with all the measures taken by Missoffe and his Ministry – sport in particular – in order to regiment them and integrate them into the state. It was symbolic for instance that early on the 'enragés' – the wild ones – of Nanterre clashed with Missoffe, when he came to open a new swimming pool.[3]

Today the Gaullist bourgeoisie has a youth policy and they are progressively going to implement it. It is truly vital for them to find the means to control the explosive potential that surfaced in the factories, work-places, colleges and schools. This policy has to be analysed and above all placed in its context. It is of utmost importance today to understand how the bourgeoisie intends to resolve the question of youth. The 'collective responsibility' of government ministers is reflected in the *complementary character of the different government measures*: on the one hand, repression and blackmail; on the other, dialogue, participation and control. The unity of Gaullist policy for youth is also reflected in the fact that the new Minister of Youth and Sport is directly attached to the Prime Minister's Office. To apply a unified policy, they have a unified conception and a unified leadership team. The bourgeois offensive against youth is thus coordinated on the basis of one overall approach. Whether it be in the universities, the Army, in the sports sector, in the local youth and culture centres, in the schools, on the beaches, in the stadiums or in the professional training centres and so on, the state seeks, in its own way, to decide the fate of young people confronted with explosive problems: selection, choice of career, police repression, mass unemployment and cultural down-grading. Gaullist demagogy with regard to sport makes sense in this context. *Repression through sport has become a matter for the state.* The state has had to bring sport into schools, not just because élite, prestige sport needs to recruit from the mass base of school and college sport, but also and most importantly, because sport is the best way of keeping control over young people.

The state's concern to develop 'sport education' can be better

3. Missoffe, Minister of Youth and Sport, declared in classic fascist style, 'If you have sexual problems, take a dip in the pool'. In other words the old clerical remedy: a cold shower to put an end to the 'temptations of the flesh' . . .

understood in the light of the role played by sport in *all* capitalist industrial states and in *all* the states under the rule of Stalinist, bureaucratic dictatorship. 'Sport', as J. Ellul rightly says, 'is a factor both for reducing the population to a mass and for exercising discipline; and in both these respects it corresponds to a totalitarian, technicist civilisation. Thus sport follows on directly from mechanised work: when a man leaves his work, sport takes over so that he is at no time independent of technique. In sport he finds the same mentality, the same criteria, the same morality, the same movements and the same objectives – all the laws and habits required by technical work organisation – which he has only just left behind him at the factory or the office.'[4] This *totalitarian 'massification'* has been studied from a general socio-political point of view by Pierre Laguillaumie. He shows synthetically the overall structural link which embeds sport in all the pores of bourgeois, capitalist industrial society, through the carceral world of exploited labour. He demonstrates the social and political necessity of 'crowd sport' (to use L. Mumford's expression) under a régime of the exploitation of man by man. In his attempt to carry out a marxist analysis of the main social and political phenomena of sport, he shows, and this is a fundamental thesis in the present context, that there are not several kinds of sport but only one: bourgeois sport. Not only does he show that the systematic organisation of sport was chronologically and structurally linked to the world-wide development of capitalist industrial society and then of imperialism, but he also shows that the typical categories, forms and constitutive principles of sport – competition, maximum output etc. – are bourgeois in character and reflect bourgeois categories. He thus shows *the world-wide social and political unity of sport* which both reflects and reinforces the political unity of bourgeois society. He therefore refuses to advance any modernist apologetics on sports culture or sport as leisure etc.

Ginette Berthaud examines the repressive aspects of sports discipline. By analysing the spirit and content of some recent experiments in sports education in schools, she shows how sports education transmits stereotyped and one-dimensional bodily techniques and is thus one of the most repressive aspects of education in a society which needs to train young people for alienated work,

4. J. Ellul, *la Technique ou l'enjeu du siècle*, Librairie A. Colin, Paris, 1954, p. 347.

to stifle their sexual needs and inculcate submission to authority. In particular, she examines the psychological mechanisms by which repression is imprinted on the individual. Using Freudian concepts, she shows how sport is an effective way of channelling energies which may become dangerous for the established order. Sport, she says, *is a cultivation of the body which turns the latter into a performance-producing machine. It is a cultivation of muscular effort which makes a virtue of labour and suffering.* In this respect, and this thesis too seems of major importance, *sport is one of the strongest factors removing the element of play from bodily activity* – (*déludisation corporelle*). A child who practices a sport is no longer playing but is taking his place in a world of serious matters, sanctioned by authority. G. Berthaud thus concludes that sports education is essentially authoritarian and repressive, and fits in exactly with the industrial rationalisation of the education system going on at present.* Sport is both a constraint in itself, and a preparation for further constraints, since it removes all bodily freedom, all creative spontaneity, every aesthetic dimension and every playful impulse. As J. Ellul aptly remarks, 'We are witnessing a process whereby playfulness and joy, contact with air and water, improvisation and spontaneity are disappearing: all these things are abandoned in favour of obedience to strict rules, efficiency and record times. Training turns men into efficient machines who know no joy other than the grim satisfaction of mastering and exploiting their own bodies.'[5]

In denouncing the sado-masochistic character of the relations between the individual and his or her body, this critique must necessarily go on to condemn the social, institutional status of the body in present-day society. François Gantheret has applied himself to the analysis, from the point of view of institutional psycho-analysis, of the dialectic between the individual, fantasised body, and the 'social body', or more exactly, of repressive institutions underpinned by determinate production relations. He has made use of his clinical experience to analyse the significance as reactions and fantasies of certain muscular practices and physical exercises which are frequently engaged in, not just by pre-psycho-

*This is a reference to the Fouchet Plan, a reform of the university and higher education system undertaken by Fouchet, the Gaullist minister for Education for 1967-68.
  5. Op. cit., p. 347. Although his political positions (defence and justi-

tics but also by 'normal' people.[6] He shows how contradictions between the organisation of society and an individual's drives are worked out in the body, particularly at the time when œdipal conflicts re-emerge during puberty. The conclusion that follows should give cause for reflection to those physical education teachers whose zeal for repressing young people is proportional to their ignorance on these questions: all social practices involving the body, all action on the body within a definite institutional framework, in this case the physical and sports education system, necessarily raise the question of the destiny of the instinctual drives, to use Freud's expression. This question is posed at three levels.

The first of these is at the level of the institutionalised initiation structures, which represent the social resolution of sub-conscious conflicts, the normalisation of fantasies, or in short, to adopt F. Gantheret's expression, a selective 'system of neuroses'. The present sports system with its personnel and field of recruitment, its prevalent modes of organisation etc. constitutes in various ways a particular 'culture medium' for breeding cultural neuroses, character types and choices of activity which F. Gantheret concurs with G. Berthaud in describing as sado-masochistic.

The second level is that of *the social perception of the body*: the theoretical understanding of the body which results in practical choice. Now, the mechanistic, Stakhanovite, behaviourist view (the 'scientific' Pavlovian reflex theory) goes with a practice of sport which treats the body as an 'animal machine'. This view of things totally excludes any understanding of the real problems as they are posed by Freudianism. If the body is really to be conceived of as a non-sexual domain, as just a bunch of muscles or at best a rather superior nervous system, as most trainers seem to think, it is obvious that the range of problems involved in the destiny of instinctual drives is no longer posed. From that point on, the only problems posed are *technical ones*: how to run faster, jump higher etc. 'Science' then becomes a smokescreen which

fication of 'Western' civilisation) are openly reactionary and his social theorisations are highly suspect ('technicist civilisation' etc.), in the case of sport, J. Ellul puts his finger on a series of partial truths which are worth recalling. As Lenin said, it is a paradoxical fact that conservative bourgeois ideologists sometimes, without realising it, uncover the reality they are supposed to be concealing.

6. *Réductions Corporelle des fonctions mentales*, Edition Sociales Françaises, Paris, 1965.

enables teachers to avoid raising the real problems posed by their status as *technocrats of the body.*

Finally, there is the level of means and methods. If, as F. Gantheret argues, the body is really *a symbolic mediation between individual fantasies and institutions,* it is also at the centre of *a transferral relation* in which all the problems of œdipal identification, substitutions and fantasy projections are to be found. We can legitimately wonder whether the physical education teacher is not in reality pursuing an objective other than his declared wish to educate young people. At this level, especially clear in the case of relationships between the champion and his trainer, we encounter the father-figure syndrome, the homosexual character of friendships in sport, the narcissism of teachers who forget that they themselves were once taught, the question of *models of bodily identification etc.*

Freud, in *Civilisation and its Discontents,* wrote that the body was one of the three sources of human unhappiness (together with the absence of mastery of nature, and the scarcity and inadequacy of human relationships). While taking this proposition as a starting point it can be shown that the body is determined not, as Freud thought, by anatomy, but rather by politics. *The body is a social set-up, given meaning by social relations,* and hence by the social structure of the time. The body is a *social institution* which has to be understood in its functional relations with other institutions. Lévi-Strauss, echoing Mauss, noted that 'each society imposes on the individual a rigorously determined utilisation of his or her body'.[7] We therefore have to try to analyse synthetically the main features of the way the body is developed under a capitalist régime, or in other words, to work out the *socio-cultural status* of *the body* in the 'leisure civilisation' and mass culture which have made a fetish of the body. To give an account of the reasons which explain the increasing reification of the body first as labour power then as a reproductive force and finally as an abstract potential consumer, requires a critique of all forms of leisure activity, amusements, distractions and would-be culture which claim to contribute to the development of the body and the creation of the 'complete man' so often referred to by the ideologists of leisure. This paves the way for a political critique of all ideological theories

7. M. Mauss, *Sociologie et Anthropologie,* PUF, Paris, 1960, introduction page XI.

about leisure, mass culture etc.

Such a political critique, from the point of view of the revolutionary proletariat, has been attempted by Michel Bhussy, taking as his theme one of the most typical models: the PCF, which recent events have once again shown up as a defender of the bourgeois order. He analyses the conceptions of the PCF with regard to leisure activities and sport, along with the policies of a PCF front organisation, the FSGT (La Fédération Sportive et Gymnastique du Travail), which aspires to occupy the Ministry of Youth and Sport in a future labour-'union-of-popular-and-democratic-forces' government. He shows in detail how the PCF's policy towards young people reflects its general policy of a peaceful and parliamentary road to socialism in the framework of peaceful co-existence. As a Party of order, the PCF does not have a revolutionary political line to offer to young people and thus inevitably falls back on 'culture', sport and leisure activities. The May revolution was a total confirmation of the revolutionary perspective developed by Michel Bhussy through his critique of the PCF – namely the need to organise the revolutionary wing of the proletariat and youth into a fighting vanguard of the working class as a whole for the socialist revolution. We should not be fighting for the 'right to sport', he says, for the task of revolutionary young people is to harness their energies to the building of a revolutionary workers' Party. The cultural agitation carried out in particular by college and school students should, he concludes, include propaganda and struggle against sport and regimentation, with the aim of freeing youth from the grip of state control.

That, briefly, is the content of this issue which has a primarily *political* unity. As the young revolutionaries constantly declared: 'This is only a start – the struggle goes on!' This issue was written from that perspective, and it should be read in the same spirit.

Jean-Marie Brohm, August 1968.

Theses Towards a Political Sociology of Sport*

1. Sport and Imperialism

(a) The Origins of Modern Sport

Modern sport, organised into national and international sports federations, is an *imperialist phenomenon*, in the marxist sense of the term. Sport developed in this form essentially from 1880-1900 onwards, in other words, at the beginning of the age of imperialism, analysed by Lenin.

The first modern Olympic games were held in Athens in 1896 and then in Paris in 1900, while the first major sports competitions such as the Tour de France or the FA Cup were organised at around the same time. Sport was directly linked to the interests of imperialist capital. The early Olympic games, in Paris, Saint-Louis and London, were organised in conjunction with Universal Exhibitions or Trade Fairs.

(b) The Organisation of Sport

From the start, the international organisation of sport was tied to imperialist international organisations. Sport served as both a supportive institution and as an ideological cover. Following both the 1914-18 and the 1939-45 World Wars, the organisation of international sport benefited from imperialist attempts to control the world. Since then, international sport has been inextricably linked to super-national organisations, in particular the UN and UNESCO. Today, the Olympic Movement and the IOC (International Olympic Committee) are closely tied to the UN and

*This is an expanded version of an article which first appeared in *Le Chrono Enrayé* No. 8 (May-June 1972).

more specifically to US Imperialism. Brundage, the President, is American [This article was written in 1971—Ed.]. Within the framework of peaceful coexistence, the International Olympic Movement fully reflects the interests of imperialism. The cosmopolitan, 'pacifist' ideology expressed in the Olympic ideal is in reality none other than the hypocritical ideology of imperialism, which 'leads to war, as surely as the storm clouds lead to the storm'.

The set-up of world sport is not just held together by its own ideology of 'peace between peoples' and by its own organisation. For imperialist sport is closely dependent on imperialist institutions and treaties such as NATO, SEATO etc. There are very close links between civilian and military sport. For instance, Western military sport is tied directly to NATO and constitutes a spearhead of North-Atlantic imperialism. The international organisation of sport constitutes a 'World Government of Sport', responsible for:

- organising international competitions,
- dealing with relations between national federations,
- laying down rules for different sports and supervising their application, settling disputes, deciding sanctions etc.,
- recognising world records,
- developing an ideological Charter for 'universal sport'.

(c) Sport and Peaceful Coexistence

As an international reality, sport is a very *precise reflection of the relation of forces between imperialism and the bureaucratic state-bourgeoisie of the 'socialist' countries* (or to use Trotskyist terminology, the Stalinist bureaucracy).

In 1921, at the Third Congress of the Communist International, a 'Red Sports International' was set up, with the aim of organising working-class sportsmen and women against the bourgeoisie. For a whole period, the USSR refused to establish sporting relations with the imperialist countries. But following the stalinisation of the USSR and the adoption of the counter-revolutionary policy of 'socialism in one country' and 'peaceful coexistence', the USSR established sporting relations with more and more countries, particularly following the end of the Second World War.

In 1952, one year before Stalin's death, the USSR took part in the Helsinki games, thereby coming into the Olympic Movement. Since that time, world sport and the Olympic games have been regarded by both the imperialist states and by the Stalinist, bureaucratic states as an important element of peaceful coexistence. The Olympic sports ideology is a hypocritical ideology which seeks to hide the reality of the class struggle behind so-called 'brotherhood between the peoples'. The reality behind the 'peace' of the sports field or the 'truce' of the Games is that sport is a grim analogue of the permanent state of war under imperialism, as can be seen by looking at the recent Olympics.

Thus the Olympic games in Melbourne in 1956 were unable to conceal the fact that the French and British imperialists were in the course of intervening in favour of the Zionist imperialists of the state of Israel with their Suez adventure. At the same time, tanks sent by the Russian Stalinist bureaucracy were bloodily crushing the revolution of the workers' councils in Hungary.

Then in 1968, all the imperialist countries sent their Olympic teams to Mexico, shortly after the Diaz Ordaz government had had student demonstrators shot down. Earlier that year, the Stalinist bureaucracy had betrayed the great general strike of May and June in France, while American imperialism was bombing, burning and killing in Vietnam. Meanwhile, the troops of the Red Army and the Warsaw Pact were invading Czechoslovakia to put down the Czech intellectuals and workers and smash the popular mobilisation of the Prague Spring.

On a world scale, sport has always been linked to the twists and turns of the international class struggle. And sport itself, notably the Olympic Movement, is an important ideological element in this struggle.

2. Bourgeois Sport and the Capitalist State

(a)   All the structures of present-day sport tie it to bourgeois, capitalist society.

Sport is dependent on the development of the productive forces of bourgeois society. Technical progress in sport closely follows the technological and scientific development of capitalism. Bourgeois sport is a class institution, totally integrated into the framework of capitalist production relations and class relations. Like other class institutions, such as the University, the Army etc.

And finally, as a phenomenon of the superstructure, sport is linked to all the other superstructural levels of capitalist society. The organisational unity of sport is ensured by the repressive grip of the bourgeois state. Moreover, sport as an ideology, transmitted on a huge scale by the mass media, is part and parcel of ruling bourgeois ideology.

(b) Sport and the State

From the start, the development of sport has been tied to that of the state. Like all other class institutions and structures, sport is mediated through the state which locks in all the structures of society as a whole. When the process of establishing bourgeois nation-states has been set in train by bourgeois revolutions such as the French Revolution of 1789, *sport has tended to participate in the process of development of these states.*

Most major national liberation movements which have fought for the establishment of nation-states have consciously made use of physical activities and mass sport *as a means of creating a national identity.*

First Example: *Jahn*[1] and anti-Napoleonic, German nationalism – the establishment of a German nationalist movement, leading to the national unification of Germany under Prussian rule.

Second Example: Mao Tse-Tung, whose early work, 'A Study of Physical Education', was to help to strengthen Chinese youth physically and mentally in the struggle against Western Imperialism and local, feudal reaction.[2] Physical education was thus a factor in the process of the bourgeois democratic revolution.

Third Example: Today all colonial and semi-colonial countries which achieve independence *structure the population by means of mass, State-run sport,* as an integral part of the establishment of their nation-state.

In situations where the state dominates all political existence, as under fascist or military/police régimes, or under the dictatorship of a Stalinist, bureaucratic state-bourgeoisie, sport is simply a

---

1. On this question see: J. Ulmann, *De la Gymnastique aux Sports Modernes*, PUF, Paris, 1965, pp. 277 on.
2. One can find some extract and a commentary of this text in S. R. Schram, *The Political Thought of Mao Tse-Tung*, Penguin Books, London, 1969, pp. 152-160.

structural part of the state repressive apparatus, particularly the army.

In this type of state, mass sport is merely a para-state institution for regimenting youth, which operates along with other reception organisations such as state-controlled youth movements, Scouts, the army etc. This was the set-up, for example, in Hitler's Germany, Stalinist Russia or in France under the Vichy régime. In this case the basic political functions of sport are:

- to control youth activities,
- ideological regimentation,
- pre-military training on nationalist lines: preparation for the 'defence of the fatherland'.

In the period of the death-agony of imperialism, bourgeois states tend increasingly to become strong, police-states, like for example the De Gaulle/Pompidou régime. In this case too, sport shares the general aims of the bourgeois state, in the widest sense of the term: sport becomes *State Sport*:

- sports structures, federations, clubs etc., are closely tied into the state apparatus;
- the state itself promotes state sport through a state doctrine: an official approach to sport which is enforced by the creation of a special administrative structure: the Ministry of Youth and Sport;
- top ranking sportsmen and women are state athletes with the job of promoting the state's official propaganda;
- the state imposes competitive sport in schools as the compulsory mode of physical education.

(c) *Sport and the capitalist organisation of production*

Sport as an activity characteristic of bourgeois industrial society, is an exact reflection of capitalist categories. And as Marx explained,[3] economic categories reflect the structures and principles of

3. 'Just as in general when examining any historical or social science, so also in the case of the development of economic categories is it always necessary to remember that the subject, in this context contemporary bourgeois society, is presupposed both in reality and in the mind, and that therefore categories express forms of existence – and sometimes merely separate aspects – of this particular society, the subject; (. . .) This has to be remembered because it provides important criteria for the arrangement of the material.' Karl Marx, *Introduction to a Critique of Political Economy*, in *The German Ideology*, part I, Lawrence & Wishart, London, 1970, p. 146.

organisation of the capitalist mode of production. The vertical, hierarchical structure of sport models the social structure of bureaucratic capitalism, with its system of competitive selection, promotion, hierarchy and social advancement. The driving forces in sport – performance, competitiveness, records – are directly carried over from the driving forces of capitalism: productivity, the search for profit, rivalry and competitiveness.

Sport as a technology of the body structurally reproduces capitalist repressive techniques: the division of labour, ultra-specialisation, repetition, training, the abstraction of space and time, stereotyped movements, the parcelling up of the body, measurement, stop-watch timing, Taylorism, Stakhanovism. . . .

Sport treats the human organism as a machine, in the same way as the worker becomes a mere appendage of the machine in the capitalist system.[4] Sport as an ideology reproduces and strengthens the ideology of alienated labour: work, continuous effort, struggle, the cult of transcending one's own limitations, the cult of suffering, the cult of self-denial, self-sacrifice etc. Sport is a morality of effort which conditions people for the oppressive work of the factory.

(d) Sport and State Monopoly Capitalism

(i) Sport as an activity involving the circulation of money and capital is thus totally tied up in the financial and economic network of monopoly capitalism. Professional sport with its show-business, its betting and its financial speculation, is just the most glaring aspect of this process.

(ii) Trusts, banking groups and monopolies use major international competitions to reinforce their domination, as for example, in the skiing events at the Grenoble Winter Olympics. Moreover major national and international competitions require huge mobilisations of capital and economic resources: thus the choice of site for the Olympic Games is the object of fierce competition between multi-national firms.

4. 'Owing to the extensive use of machinery and to division of labour, the work of the proletarians has lost all individual character, and, consequently, all charm for the workman. He becomes an appendage of the machine, and it is only the most simple, most monotonous, and most easily acquired knack, that is required of him.' K. Marx and F. Engels, *Manifesto of the Communist Party*, in K. Mark/F. Engels, *Collected Works*, Vol. 6, Lawrence and Wishart, London, 1975, p. 490-91.

(iii) Sport also develops its own industries on a broad, capitalist basis, through the manufacture of equipment and the promotion of sporting goods. Financial trusts, such as Rothschild, were quick to develop and profit from the sports and leisure industry, Winter Sports and the 'Club Méditerranée'.

(e) Sport and capitalist Showbusiness

Spectator sport is a commodity sold along normal capitalist lines. Sportsmen and women themselves are commodities, bought and sold according to the law of supply and demand, viz. the famous 'transfers' of professional footballers.

As soon as spectator sport becomes caught up in the capitalist web, the door is inevitably open to every kind of 'abuse' and 'fiddle': shamateurism, the star-system and the hunt for high fees.

As a form of mass entertainment, sport is a process whereby the population is reduced to an ideological mass. Sport is a means of regimentation and de-humanisation – see, for example, the role of football in Brazil, Britain or Spain, or of cycling in Italy and France, or of baseball in the USA etc. Spectator sports are a mass political safety-valve, a system of social diversion and an element in pre-military conditioning. Moreover, it is worth noting that most major competitions are controlled, if not actually run, by the police and the army, as was the case at the Mexico and Grenoble Games. In other words sport, as one of the factors for maintaining law and order, is usually controlled by the forces of law and order.

The ceremonies at major sports competitions are just like big military parades or pre-fascist rallies, with their 'traditional' or military music, the flag rituals, rhythmic marches, national anthems and medal ceremonies. The best examples of this kind of ceremonial are provided by the Hitlerite Games of 1936 in Berlin and the Mexico Games, controlled by the same *Granaderos* who had taken part in the repression of the student movement.

(f) Sport and the ruling ideology

Sport is a concentrated form, an officially promoted microcosm, of all the ideological prejudices of bureaucratic, bourgeois society:
- the cult of the champion and the star-system;
- the cult of promotion, social advancement and the hierarchy;
- the myth of transcending one's own limitations through effort;

52

- character building;
- sexual repression – the healthy life etc.;
- the brotherhood of man – everyone united on the sports-field;
- nationalism and chauvinism.

3. Institutional Repression

* Sport is a social process for the continuous repression of child-hood drives. As a socialising institution, sport channels the sexual drives of the adolescent in a repressive direction, through sublima-tion, unconscious repression and diversion.

* As Freud showed, sport replaces libidinal pleasure with the masochistic pleasure obtained from movement. As sports trainers are constantly stressing: 'It's when it hurts that it's doing you good!'

* Sport is a process whereby codified, stereotyped 'bodily tech-niques' are imprinted with the aim of producing automatic, adap-tive reflexes.

* Sport is the repressive cultural codification of movements.

* Sport helps to shape the super-ego of the adolescent: external repression is internalised through the mediation of the trainer, the representative of bourgeois values and the bourgeois social order.

* *Sport is alienating. It will disappear in a universal communist society.*

Jean-Marie Brohm, April 1971.

Sport, an Ideological State Apparatus: The Neutrality of the Sports-field*

Sport is everywhere. The mass media are saturated with sports reports and the results of sports competitions; Heads of State give receptions for champions in their palaces; sport is found in every sector of the social formation, whether it be the school, the Army or the factory. Major sporting events attract huge crowds. In short, in all 'developed societies', whether 'liberal' capitalist, or bureaucratic state-capitalist, sport is a *mass phenomenon*. Yet, surprisingly, neither marxist nor positivist sociology has serious-ly attempted to analyse this phenomenon. Is sport then just a for-gotten area? No, it is an unconsciously *repressed* area. The insti-tution of sport is a real blind-spot and is thus screened off from view: there is a consensus to conceal its function and its socio-political significance.

We are told that sport is universal, above all conflicts between races and nations. Certainly all nations are unanimous in their eagerness to take part in the 'festival of youth, friendship and peace' at the great masquerade of the Olympic games. China is the only nation so far refusing to participate in this mystification, though the ping-pong diplomacy so dear to the 'Great Helms-man', and the search for respectability seem to be leading the Chinese to succumb to this latest form of conformism. Sport is 'neutral': it has nothing to do with the class struggle. That is what 'common sense' tells us, and, as Engels said, common sense is 'the worst kind of metaphysics'. Even when the *Charléty* stadium was chosen as the venue for the mass meeting where the

---

*This is a re-worked version of an article in *Politique aujourd'hui* (Ideology and cultural production), October-December 1974.

workers' official leaders tried to regain control of the French general strike in May '68, no one was led to question such a *political use of the space of a stadium*. However, since that time the apparent neutrality of the stadium has been drowned in the blood of our Chilean comrades.[1]

In May 1968, none of the revolutionary criticism was directed against sport. Sport did not experience the generalised 'institutional trance', to use an expression coined by my friend René Lourau. Why did the 'negation process' pass sport by? Why, on the contrary, did the apparatus of the CGT [Confédération Générale du Travail, the largest of the three French trade union federations, Ed.] and the Communist Party encourage strikers to be diverted by music and sport (diverted from what? we might ask). How can the universal neglect of this problem by the far-left be explained?[2] Undoubtedly all these questions can only be answered by analysing the role of sports ideology and the reasons for its predominance.

1. Sports Ideology

The sports system in general appears as an 'armed apparatus of coercion', to use Gramsci's term, which has the ultimate function of protecting the class rule of the bourgeoisie. Sport, like all other institutions, is mediated through the structures of the State appara-

1. During the occupation of France, Jews were interned in the cycling stadium, the *'Vel' d' Hiv'* '. See also the revelations in *Libération* about the plans made by the French secret service and the Gaullist para-police organisation, the SAC, to intern working class militants in the Marseilles sports stadiums in May '68.

2. The only critical writings in French can be found in the following works: *Partisans*, *'Sport, culture et répression'*, Maspéro Paris, 1972, with articles by G. Berthaud, P. Laguillaumie, F. Gantheret and J.-M. Brohm; D. Robert: *La signification du 'vrai' sport à l'école*, an *Ecole Emancipée* pamphlet, Paris, 1969; J.-M. Brohm, C. Maurin and J.-M. Damian: *l'Opium Olympique*, in *Politique Hebdo* No. 43 (7.9.72); *Le Chrono Enrayé*, the review of the *Ecole Emancipée*, 2 issues on the Munich Olympics, April and September, 1972; J.-M. Brohm, *'Vers l'analyse institutionnelle du sport de compétition'*, in *l'Homme et la Société*, Nos. 29-30, 1973. The following German writings should also be mentioned: G. Vinnai, *Fussballsport als Ideologie*, Europaïsche Verlagsanstalt, Frankfurt/Main, 1970; U. Prokop, *Soziologie der Olympischen Speile*, Hanser Verlag, Munich 1971; Böhme, Gadow, et. al., *Sport im Kapitalismus*, Limpert, Frankfurt/Main, 1972; G. Vinnai, et. al., *Sport in der Klassengesellschaft*, Fischer Verlag, Frankfurt/ Main, 1972. And now also: J.-M. Brohm, *Sociologie politique du sport*, Editions Universitaires, Paris, 1976.

tus, which means that it takes on a political form.[3] Sport is also an instrument of bourgeois hegemony, in the Gramscian sense of the word, that is to say it is one of those secondary arms of the state which enable 'one social group to exercise its hegemony over national society as a whole . . . through organisations such as the Church, the trade-unions, political parties, the schools etc.'[4] Thus, if sport, like the above institutions, is an 'apparatus of civil hegemony', or, to adopt Althusser's expression, an 'ideological state apparatus', it too functions thanks to ideology.[5] How?

Sports ideology, like all ideologies, *veils* the real structure of production relations which it assumes as 'natural'. This ideology *masks* class relations by turning the relations between the individuals within the sporting institution into material relations between things: scores, machines, records, human bodies treated as commodities and so on.[6] The ideology would have it that sportsmen and women are formally free and equal, which then justifies their being ranked into different grades. The hero of this ideology is the 'self-made man' who attains the heights of performance on the basis of his own merit and through his own efforts: social advancement is possible after all . . .

Sports ideology, like all ideology, contributes to the enlarged reproduction of the social relations of production.

Firstly, sport trains the work-force to operate according to the norms of capitalist, or bureaucratic state-capitalist exploitation. Sport is basically a mechanisation of the body, treated as an automaton, governed by the principle of maximising output. The organism is trained to sustain prolonged effort and maintain the necessary regularity of pace. J. Habermas notes the close similarity between production-line work and the process of training for sport. In the guise of a game which is supposed to freely develop the strengths of the individual, sport in fact reproduces the world of

3. K. Marx and F. Engels, *The German Ideology*, in K. Marx/F. Engels, *Collected Works*, Vol. 5, Lawrence & Wishart, London, 1975, p. 90.
4. A. Gramsci, *Oeuvres choisies*, ed. Sociales, Paris, 1959, p. 30.
5. L. Althusser, *Ideology and Ideological State apparatuses* in *Lenin and Philosophy, and other essays*, NLB, London 1971, pp. 121-173.
6. We find here again the concept of 'Commodity fetishism' that is to say, according to Marx, 'a definite social relation between men themselves which assumes here, for them, the fantastic form of a relation between things.' *Capital* Vol. I, Penguin Books, London, 1976, p. 165.

work.[7] B. Rigauer expands the point: 'In both cases . . . we find the same general characteristic: different tasks, allotted to standardised work-stations, are carried out in continuous succession. . . .'[8] Mechanical techniques, involving the automatic performance of broken-down training routines and the systematic inculcation of effort and resistance to pain, are the general rule in sport. Some swimmers put in up to 20 kilometres a day, runners do up to 50 kilometres, while weight-lifters lift several tons. We can accept Adorno's conclusion that 'Sport restores to mankind some of the functions which the machine has taken away from him, but only to regiment him remorselessly in the service of the machine'.[9] In Eastern Europe, sport is systematically conceived in terms of labour. An official apologist, W. Spieger, explains: 'The science of sport is a general and systematic study of human development and the simple and enlarged reproduction of man as labour-power.' He then proposes the term 'humanics', for this 'science of the best form of human life, this science of human output'.[10] As Stalin put it, man is 'the most precious capital of all . . .'

2. Sexual Discipline

It is mainly through the repressive sublimation of sexual drives that the practice of competitive sport contributes to the reproduction of the social relations of production. Indeed this repression is necessary for the stability of production relations, for the enlarged reproduction and rationalisation of labour power, the productivity of which determines the extraction of surplus value. Gramsci, whose views on the subject anticipate the work of the 'Freudian Marxists', wrote: 'These new methods (of work) require a rigid discipline of the sexual instincts, of the nervous system, which implies a strengthening of the "family", understood in the broad sense . . . of a system for regulating and stabilising sexual

7. J. Habermas, 'Soziologische Notizen zum Varhältnis con Arbeit und Freizeit', in Konkrete Vernunft, Bonn, 1958, p. 227.
8. B. Rigauer, Sport und Arbeit, Suhrkamp, Frankfurt/Main 1969, p. 34.
9. Th. W. Adorno, Prismen, Kulturkritik und Gesellschaft, Frankfurt/Main, 1955, p. 76 (our emphasis).
10. W. Sieger, 'L'éducation physique dans la société socialiste et communiste', in Recherches internationales à la lumière du marxisme, No. 48, 1965, p. 131.

relations.'[11] The family is the key institution for the reproduction of social relations. Within what Reich called 'this miniature State', the child learns the future behaviour patterns of work and obedience. Through the super-ego, the child internalises the bourgeois morality of work and efficiency. In the family, the child assimilates the ethical structures of civil society and learns to control his drives – 'The morality of the sphincter muscles,' comments S. Ferenszi. Gramsci adds: 'The new industrialism requires monogamy – the worker must not waste his nervous energy in the random and distracting search for casual sexual satisfaction.' *The whole system therefore requires the sexual Taylorisation of the body.*

Two repressive processes come into play. First, specifically erotic pleasure has to be replaced by pleasure in muscular movement. 'Modern education', wrote Freud, 'makes great use of games in order to divert young people from sexual activity. It would be more correct to say that in these young people it replaces sexual enjoyment by pleasure in movement – and forces sexual activity back to one of its auto-erotic components'.[12] The second, more 'sporting' repressive process consists in the cultivation of a sado-masochistic type of personality, which enables the individual to relish his own physical pain. To be convinced of this, you simply have to watch certain events such as the marathon, in which confronting and overcoming pain almost becomes a drug. Alain Mimoun, the marathon runner, himself admitted as much! *In short, sport 'changes libidinal potential into a potential for work',[13] and turns the 'love-body' into a 'labouring body'.*

3. Order and Hierarchy

The ideology of sport transmits hierarchical, élitist and authoritarian values. The system forms a pyramid, in which those at the top are supposed to be 'guides for the human race', as a sports expert of the French CP put it. *This pyramid displays the main characteristics of the bureaucratic system.* By going through this mill, this miniature hierarchy, adolescents are taught a sense of

11. A. Gramsci, *Oeuvres choisies*, op. cit., p. 410.
12. S. Freud, *Three Essays on the Theory of Sexuality*, The Hogarth Press, London 1962, p. 69 note (2).
13. M. Bonaparte, *Introduction à la théorie des instincts*, PUF, Paris, 1951, p. 92.

58

the social hierarchy which sport trains them to accept. As Bourdieu and Passeron, analysing the academic world, write:

'. . . the apparently purely academic cult of hierarchy always contributes to the defence and legitimation of social hierarchies, because academic hierarchies, whether of degrees and diplomas or establishments and disciplines, always owe something to the social hierarchies which they tend to re-produce (in both senses). So it has to be asked whether the freedom the educational system is given to enforce its own standards and its own hierarchies (. . .), is not the quid pro of the hidden services it renders to certain classes *by concealing social selection under the guise of technical selection and legitimating the reproduction of the social hierarchies by transmuting them into academic hierarchies*'.[14]

This analysis is entirely applicable to the sports system. A striking example of the ideology of social advancement is to be found in the official *Draft Sports Doctrine*, written under the auspices of a former member of the Vichy Régime, Borotra:

'Sport is often what binds a group together – a highly cohesive structure which banishes social barriers and differences and is based on the equality of all. . . . Sport satisfies the need for social participation and brings into being a parallel hierarchy, alongside the hierarchy which most people have imposed on them in everyday life. This parallel hierarchy takes no account of people's everyday status and gives them opportunities for achievement which they are denied by modern society.'[15]

By creating this illusory hierarchy, sport fulfils a compensatory and diversionary function. Its make-believe equality serves to avoid doing anything about 'the hierarchy of everyday life'. Moreover, the practice of sport inculcates an attitude of submission to the established order. From this point of view, effort, sportsmanship, discipline and above all, self-denial are an excellent school. The *Draft Doctrine*, this ideological mish-mash, makes no bones about it, and in the vein of '*Sport machte frei*', sings the praises of 'the necessity for rules and the benefits of disinterested, organised

14. P. Bourdieu and J.-C. Passeron, *Reproduction: In Education, Society and Culture*, Sage Publications, London and Beverly Hills, 1977, pp. 152-153 (our emphasis).
15. Published by the Haut Comité des Sports, Paris, 1965, p. 20.

effort'.[16] Better still, sport has the advantage of diverting young people away from revolt against the bourgeois order. As the 'Draft' puts it:

'Sport prevents the development of many of the modern symptoms of dissatisfaction among young people, torn between their aspirations and their fears for the future. The questioning of traditional values allows them to escape the moral constraints which are just as indispensable today as ever. The inadequate attention they receive at home and school leaves them to their own devices and, egged on by the example of the disorders of present day society, which are obligingly dangled in front of their eyes, they turn to forms of action based on defiance and force. Sport is a source of happiness for young people which helps to develop a healthy, vigorous and dynamic type of man, aware both of his own value and of his own limitations.'[17]

4. The Keynote: Competition

The ideological apparatus of sport has, of course, other functions which it is not possible to describe here. For example, mention should be made of the *sporting world-view* with its champions and idols, of the way sport structures the relationship between man and his body, etc.

The sports system is a sediment made up of several ideological layers, which have a natural place in everyday life. That is because this ideology, which it is our task to demolish, corresponds exactly to the norms according to which capitalist, industrial society functions.[18]

Sports ideology is the direct reflection of the competition between sportsmen and women who compare their performances (their 'commodities') on the 'market' of records and sporting achievements. This ideology of sporting competition corresponds to capitalist competition, which 'spreads into every kind of activity and intrudes into love, play and all other social relations'.[19] In

16. Op. cit., p. 24.
17. Op. cit., p. 23.
18. Cf. C. Graf von Krockow, *'Der Wetteifer in der industriellen gesell-schaft und im Sport'*, in *Der Wetteifer*, W. Limpert Verlag, Frankfurt/ Main, 1962.
19. K. Horney, *La personnalité névrotique de notre temps*, L'Arche, Paris, 1953, p. 127.

capitalist society, everything is a commodity. Thus the essence of all activity is *the comparison, within a homogenous framework* such as the market, the Courts, the sports-field or the Stock Exchange etc. of rates of profit, quantities of labour, commodities, monetary symbols, crimes and prison sentences,[20] sexual 'exploits' (which have their own 'Olympic Games') and, last but not least, sports records.

The ideology of competition expresses this constant comparative activity. According to the 'Official Instructions', issued to French Physical Education teachers, 'competition is one of the foundations of our civilisation'. Obviously free-enterprise is the institution at the root of this ideology, as of many others. Marx wrote: '. . . Darwin recognises among beasts and plants his English society with its division of labour, competition, opening up of new markets, "inventions" and the Malthusian "struggle for existence".'[21] Along the same lines, G. Magnane notes that 'the need for people to prove themselves through competition is still the key-note of Western culture. The principle of free-enterprise gives it official sanction'.[22] Even elections are treated as 'matches', decided by 'scores' which lead to the 'KO'. Industrial firms achieve 'records', Finance Ministers have 'rounds' of talks, and even love is increasingly identified with 'sexual gymnastics'.

The *positivism* of capitalist societies can clearly be seen in the Saint-Simonist ideology of sport. As a physical education teacher naïvely put it: 'We are left speechless in face of the constant bettering of performances.'[23] Human progress is thus to be measured in terms of the constant improvement of records. In this field, *time* is one of the key themes. Time in sport is a smooth, descending curve. In sport you are always running against the clock. The stop-watch is the symbol of this process of quantification. A group of militant PE teachers chose an apt title for their publication: they stood the symbol on its head by calling their review 'The Stopped Stop-Watch', and they took as their watchword, the destruction of the 'instruments of sporting alienation'. Another constantly recurring theme is the notion of human physical

20. Cf. E. Pashukanis, *Law and Marxism – A General Theory*, Ink Links, London, 1978.
21. K. Marx, *Letter to Engels* of 18.6.1862, in K. Marx/F. Engels, *Selected Correspondence*, Lawrence & Wishart, London, 1956, p. 156.
22. G. Magnane, *Sociologie du sport*, Idées, Gallimard, Paris, 1964, p. 31.
23. Review: *Education Physique et Sport*, No. 52.

progress, as measured by performances. This idea, which the Nazis put to service to 'improve their race', frequently appears in sports reviews, where the performances of black, yellow and white peoples are compared. J. Rouyer, a spokesman for the French CP, declared: 'the educability of man seems limitless. The capacity of man to go beyond his own limitations can be measured in the specific field of sports records. Even the myth of biological stability has been exploded.'[24] Furthermore, for the French CP, the theme of progress is tied to that of competition, since 'the ideal of going beyond one's own limitations, of pushing back the frontiers of human capacity is the basic driving force behind the practice of sport. And this ideal inevitably gives rise to top-level competition'.[25]

5. Productivity first

Sport is the experimental science of human productivity.[26] The same idea is expressed in another way by B. Rigauer, when he notes that 'the principles of capitalist, commercial society structurally determine sport'.[27] Competition implies that the maximum possible productivity be extracted from the labour-power of sportsmen and women, that is to say, from their capacity for high performance. The main preoccupation is to discover the best way of identifying future champions, to promote the most effective training methods, in short, to develop a kind of *sporting mode of production* of the kind that can be seen in East Germany. At this point we should include a word of warning against the illusions that abound on this question in the Communist Party, in many far-left groups and elsewhere. It is an illusion to think that in a socialist society it will be enough to separate the wheat from the chaff, to rid sport of its accompanying 'abuses' and 'excesses' for it to become 'educative', humane and 'progressive'. Once you accept the principle of maximum productivity, all the consequences, such as the obsession with champions, necessarily follow. It should

24. J. Rouyer, 'Recherches sur la signification humaine du sport et du loisir', in Recherches internationales à la lumière du marxisme, op. cit., p. 66.
25. 'Le Parti Communiste Français et les activités physiques et sportives', l'Ecole et la Nation, No. 180, June 1969, p. 90.
26. See L. Volpicelli, Industrialismo e sport, Armando, Rome, 1960, p. 34.
27. B. Rigauer, 'Leistungssport als Arbeitsleistung', in Die Vertrimmte Nation oder Sport in rechter gesellschaft, Rowonit, Reinbek bei Hamburg, 1972, p. 67.

also be noted that the same conception of sport prevails in countries like the USSR, Cuba or China as in the capitalist countries. The practice of competitive sport is everywhere governed by the *same* international federations, the *same* rules, the *same* techniques and the *same* training methods. That is an inevitable consequence of the principle of maximum productivity, which tends to treat the body as a cybernetic system. Far from being freed from constraints, the athlete's body is totally tied up in a network of standardised repressive techniques. Through the practice of obsessive repetition, sport leads to the *alienation of the individual*.

The sports system acts as a kind of huge distorting mirror on life and history. Sport constitutes a specific, concentrated form of a prevalent mythical structure, which is why it serves so readily as a vehicle for human fantasies. The first aspect of this mythology feeds on a constantly recurring question: *who is the best?* As German far-left militants put it:

> 'Sport is a set of monotonous variations on a single theme: the question – who is the strongest? Who can run fastest? Who can throw farthest? In other words, what organised, top-level, competitive sport, with its enormous ideological and material resources, seeks to present as an enquiry into the limits of human capacity, really boils down to this childish question.'[28]

Thus at the Munich Olympics, M. Spitz, winner of seven gold medals, was crowned 'King of the Olympics'; Merckx is called 'the greatest cyclist of all time'; Killy is described as 'the champion of champions', etc.

The other basic theme revolves around the authors of 'fabulous exploits'. The mythology needs to be tied to historical certainties. It is of the utmost importance to know who first cleared 2.30 metres in the high-jump, who ran the first 10 second 100 metres – each of these exploits represents the breaking of a symbolic barrier. 'These magic barriers are merely round figures chosen from the continuum of the relevant parameters, which provide a way of periodising history. The history of sport can only be written in terms of "The first man to . . .".'[29]

28. H. H. Henschen and R. Wetter, *Anti-Olympia*, Reihe Hanser Verlag, Munich, 1972, p. 16.
29. H. H. Henschen *et al.*, op cit., p. 21.

6. Ultimate madness

The last of these themes is the completely crazy project of comparing human performances with other species. In an article in the September 1973 issue of *Paris-Match*, human beings were set alongside 'the most sporting species'. The ranking for the high-jump works out as follows: the porpoise comes first with 6 metres, followed by the puma (4.50m), the salmon (3m) and man (2.3m). The speed champion is the cheetah, at 100 kilometres an hour, in front of the hare (74 k.p.h.), and man is far behind at 37 k.p.h. Sporting vocabulary often borrows from the animal kingdom. Spitz is the 'hungry Olympic shark', whereas S. Gould becomes the 'dark mermaid'. W. Rudolph is the 'black gazelle', and a wrestler is dubbed 'the Polish bull' etc. The mass media are particularly fond of this menagerie. The mythology of sport is thus peopled with hybrids, supermen, giants and gods who fight it out in a kind of pre-historic jungle.

Our analysis of sports ideology as a state apparatus is inevitably incomplete. Many of its characteristics have not been taken up. These include the ideology of peaceful coexistence and class collaboration, the drive towards fascist-type ceremonial, the male-chauvinist, fascistic ideology of virility and the strong, tanned body-beautiful . . . Such a full analysis will undoubtedly be facilitated by *the crisis, which affects the institution of sport*, just as it touches all other ideological state apparatuses. The bourgeoisie realises this. For instance, in the financial journal *Les Informations*, we read:

'The critique (of sport) goes further: not content with attacking the political use that is sometimes made of sport . . . the far-left now condemns the very values which have been its main strengths – team spirit, the will to win, the discipline of training. These values, they claim, are simply modelled on the values of a capitalist society. Like the family, progress or hard work, sport is one of those values we thought were solid, universally accepted, politically neutral and above party quarrels. Now we find that sport in its turn has come into the rebel's line of fire.'[30]

This realisation should lead marxist-leninist militants to continue their efforts. The task is to denounce bourgeois sport as such,

30. *Les Informations*, No. 1425, 4th September, 1973.

and not to try to reform it as the revisionists propose. We have to organise a revolutionary youth movement, not to provide 'red' leisure activities for youth (as, for instance, does the AJS [Alliance de la Jeunesse Socialiste, a Trotskyist youth organisation in France, Ed.], which organises 'red' sports competitions at its summer camps). Trotsky long ago observed, 'In the sphere of *philanthropy, amusements and sports*, the bourgeoisie and the church are incomparatively stronger than we are. We cannot tear away the working class youth from them except by means of the socialist programme and revolutionary action.'[31]

Jean-Marie Brohm, October 1974.

31. L. Trotsky, *Whither France*, Pathfinder Press, New York, 1968, p. 102.

Why the 'Ecole Emancipée' is Against Competitive Sport*

Today, both in the physical and sports education sector and, more generally, in all the mass media, a fierce ideological struggle is being waged over sport. For instance, after a recent conference in Amiens, a correspondent from *Le Monde* commented on interventions by members of the *Ecole Emancipée* and members of the Communist League, noting with astonishment the rapidity with which the values of sport have been put into question.

The success of the Anti-Olympic Committee gave rise to a growing awareness of the reactionary and repressive political functions of capitalist and Stalinist sport.

The challenge is so great that M. Mazeaud [Minister for Sport in the Pompidou administration—Ed.] himself felt it necessary to cite, quite accurately, the charges made against sport, in order the better to be able to answer them.

Thus *Le Monde* of the 1st December, 1973, quotes extracts from M. Mazeaud's speech on the occasion of the 15th anniversary of the Sport and Culture Federation of France:

'1. Sport is said to turn man into a slave as an inevitable consequence of competition, which implies trying to win by whatever means: the athlete thereby becomes a victim of his own single-minded objective.

'2. Anyone who puts a foot on the slippery slope of sport cannot avoid being regimented, especially by the State which is on the look out for champions to represent it.

---

*This is an enlarged version of an article which appeared in *L'Ecole Emancipée*, No. 15, May 1974. *L'Ecole Emancipée* is a revolutionary tendency within the FEN, La Fédération de l'Education Nationale, the National Union of Teachers in France.

'3. In any case, sport is really nothing more than a reflection of industrial capitalism.

'This is held to be clearly proved by the advertising that surrounds sport and sporting events and by the growth of all the industries producing sports goods.

'The drive for greater output and the increasingly artificial environment of sport are supposed to confirm this thesis.

'4. Sport is said to be a system of diversion, a distraction in the full sense of the word, which prevents adults from facing up to their responsibilities.'

All this is somewhat surprising, and no doubt the Stalinists will be quick, as usual, to allege 'collusion' between the régime and the 'ultra-lefts'!

Recently again, a member of *Ecole Emancipée* was interviewed on commercial radio about his tendency's positions on sport. And only a few weeks ago, the *Nouvel Observateur* [a very widely read Social-Democratic weekly—Ed.] published an article which cited the positions of *Partisans* and the *Ecole Emancipée* on the subject.

So it can be seen that the *Ecole Emancipée* is at the centre of the present debate over the critique of bourgeois sport. It is therefore high time to clarify our position publicly, since we were the first, through *Partisans* and the *Chrono Enrayé*, to challenge competitive sport and its alienation.

1. For a Revolutionary Marxist Definition of Sport

One of the first difficulties in reaching agreement on the critique of sport stems from *the ambiguity, or rather the multiple meanings of the word 'sport'*.

The word is applied to activities as different as a casual game of football among mates, a Sunday morning jog, the little sprint we indulge in to catch the bus, a champion's training routine, top-level competition, sport at school, sport for all, spare-time gymnastics, relaxation sessions etc.

Coubertin provided a classic definition of sport: 'Sport is the voluntary and habitual cultivation of intensive muscular effort based on the desire for progress, which can even go to the point of taking risks.'

This definition and the many similar ones which could be quoted, are 'neutral' enough, but they do not provide us with a *dialectical materialist definition of the phenomenon of sport as a whole.*

From the point of view of revolutionary marxism, *sport is a complex system of institutionalised social practices, governed by the principles of maximum output, training, competition, and selection.*

It is characterised by:

(i)   *Competition.* 'The idea on which sport is based – its funda- mental category – is performance' writes B. Guillermain.[1] Or, as Seurin writes: 'Competition amounts to this: trying to be first (ranking); to defeat an opponent (winning); or to do better than others have been able to do in similar circumstances (records).'[2] Sport is thus a form of positivism based on measured results.

(ii)   *The notion of record.* The notion of record, which is linked to that of competition, is *central* to sport. As A. Gehlen writes: 'This notion corresponds to the constantly increasing rationalisa- tion and indeed to the scientific tendency of our time, in that it ignores questions of quality and focuses exclusively on what is measurable and quantifiable – the elements concerned must be objectively measurable and hence quantitative.'[3]

(iii)   *The sporting scale of values.* Sportsmen and women, by virtue of their activity, adopt a *sporting scale of values.* As J. Bastardy puts it: 'In sport the hierarchies are precise, strict and obvious to all. In this way the mind satisfies an elementary need for order: a world in which Bobet is the best cyclist, Zatopek the best runner and Racing Club the best team is a fine, ordered world where you feel at ease, where everything is in its place and in which you can play your part.'[4]

To sum up, we can agree with M. Bouet that 'only really organ- ised competition fully embodies the essence of competitive sport'.[5]

1.   B. Guillemain, *le Sport et l'éducation*, PUF, Paris, 1955, p. 9.
2.   P. Seurin, *'Compétition et éducation physique'*, in *l'Homme sain*, Bor- deaux, December 1961, p. 324.
3.   A. Gehlen, *'Sport und Gesellschaft'*, in *Das Grosse Spiel, Aspekte des Sports in unserer Zeit*, Fischer Verlag, Frankfurt, 1965, p. 29.
4.   J.-P. Bastardy, *Education du corps*, Fleurus, 1964, p. 54.
5.   M. Bouet, *Signification du sport*, Editions Universitaires, Paris, 1968, p. 45.

(iv) *Training: the hard labour of sport.* These days, sports training has *gone mad*. We are producing sports robots. A few figures illustrate this: Zatopek or Jazy run from 30 to 50 kilometres a day. Mark Spitz swims some 4,500 kilometres a year. An East German woman swimmer puts in 22 kilometres a day. The winner of the Gold Medal for the javelin at the Munich Olympics, Wolferman, throws the javelin 600 times a week, and lifts several tons in training during the same period.

Sports training is thus structurally similar to production line work in a factory and involves the same inhuman work pace.

(v) *The principle of maximum output.* J. Paulhac has convincingly shown that sport is dominated by an industrial conception of output:

'Without going as far as J-M. Brohm in *Partisans* of April '66, in identifying output in sport and industrial output, I cannot help being struck by the utilitarianism and the merciless selection that operates in most civilian clubs. The customary policy is to detect talented beginners, to select the most gifted of them, to whip them up with training routines that turn them into robots and then exploit their performances to build up the club's reputation.'[6]

In fact, sport is *the rational organisation of human output.* The German fascist theorist of sport, C. Diem, who was one of the organisers of the Nazi Games in Berlin in 1936, wrote: 'Maximum output . . . the search for a performance or a record . . . is the fundamental characteristic of sport.' Or as Bouet puts it: 'The competitive perspective is inherent in sport.'[7]

In other words, the distinction between top-level sport and mass sport is not a valid one, in that both are fundamentally based on the principle of maximum output. That is also why it is impossible to 'reform' sport and make it 'educative', unless of course you think the principle of maximum output can be made educative. For the principle of maximum output in sport closely reflects the principle of maximum profit which governs capitalist society.

To recapitulate, *sport is an institutionalised system of competitive, delimited, codified and conventionally governed physical*

6. *Le Monde* of 23.6.73.
7. M. Bouet, op. cit., p. 62.

practices which have the avowed aim of selecting the best compe-
petitor – the champion – or recording the best performance – the
record – on the basis of comparing performances.

Sport is thus a system of generalised physical competitions with
the objective of comparing and measuring the performances of the
human body, conceived as having a potential for unlimited
improvement.

Sport is the institutionalised positivism of physical progress.

On the institutional, superstructural level, *sport ideologically*
reproduces the world of work. It is a *symbolic parallel* of this
world. This fundamental thesis of the sociology of sport holds that
capitalist production relations are reproduced symbolically in the
relations between the participants in the sporting mode of production.

The German sociologist, A. Gehlen, writes: 'The internal structural parallel between sport and work is a fact that cannot be
denied. That is why sport is a distorted reflection of the serious
business of work.'[8] This makes it possible to understand why the
institution of sport should come into existence and develop at the
same time as the capitalist industrial mode of production in England during the 18th and 19th centuries, alongside the primitive
accumulation of capital.

The world sports system developed hand in hand with the
organisation of the capitalist world market and the spread of
imperialism and colonialism – look at the development of golf
and cricket in India for example.

One further point should be mentioned: that is the question of
the agelessness of sport. Sport is not 'as old as the hills', as P.
Vimard claims. It appeared on the scene with the capitalist mode
of production in England. In other words, present-day sport reflects totally different social relations of production from those
within which sport was practised in antiquity. Moreover, sport
in antiquity was conceived in a religious and cultural perspective –
modern sport is quite simply positivist. Finally, and most importantly, sport in antiquity had no place for systematic measurement,
precise timing, or the recognition of records.

All these reasons explain Ulmann's confidence in asserting that,
'The comparison of Greek and British sport reveals that *they differ*
in every respect. Such a comparison also shows how simplistic

8. A. Gehlen, op. cit., p. 28.

most theories of sport are. These theories set out to show that sport, in its own way, brings out permanent features of human nature.'[9]

2. The Institution of Sport

It is clear that one of the salient features of the phenomenon of sport, which is generally ignored by its apologists, is its institutional character.

Sport is an *ideological state apparatus,* that is to say, an apparatus which serves as a buffer for the state's repressive apparatus. In the context of state monopoly capitalism, sport becomes *state monopoly sport,* which can no more be 'put right' than can the state itself be 'reformed'.

Sport as an ideological state apparatus contributes to the reproduction of the social relations of production on an enlarged scale and to the spreading of the ruling ideology. It thereby serves to defend the capitalist order and bourgeois rule.

The institutional aspect of sport takes the concrete form of a *sports administration* – clubs, federations, regional organisations, Olympic Committees etc. – which on a world scale, constitute a 'world government of sport', to adopt J. Meynaud's expression,[10] closely linked to imperialist organisations like the UN, UNESCO etc.

In short, *the institution of sport reproduces* all the principles of bourgeois society *in a concentrated form.* As R. Louran puts it: 'The symbolic character of the institution resides in the fact that this one particular sector of social practice displays the general tendencies of the social system as a whole.'[11]

(a) Sport and Capitalism

(i) *Enlarged reproduction of the social relations of production.* Sport reproduces materially and symbolically the social relations of production. It both constitutes an ideological parallel of these

9. J. Ulmann, *De la gymnastique aux sports modernes,* PUF, Paris, 1965, p. 285 (our emphasis).
10. J. Meynaud, *Sport et politique,* Payot, Paris, 1966, p. 186.
11. R. Lourau, *l'Analyse institutionelle,* Editions de Minuit, Paris, 1970, p. 90.

relations and in addition serves as a cover for them. In this sense sport becomes what Gramsci called a hegemonic 'armed coercive apparatus' – a kind of carapace which ideologically binds the state together.

There is a structural parallel between the capitalist mode of production and the sporting process.

First of all, sport corresponds to a determinate level of development of the productive forces – the capitalist stage – and thus forms part of the totality of bourgeois relations of production. This is what the majority of its apologists ignore with their talk of an 'eternal essence' of sport.

Capitalist society is based on commercial war: on generalised economic competition. This competition extends into all fields. As K. Horney writes: 'From its origins in the economic field, competition spreads into every kind of activity and intrudes into love, play and all other social relations.'[12]

The structural parallel between commercial competition and competition in sport makes it possible to explain the capitalist character of sport. There is a parallel both between abstract labour and abstract performance and between labour-power, exchanged for wages, and the capacity to produce performances in sport.

Commodities have a double character: they are both use-values and exchange-values. For exchange-value to be quantified, there must be an element common to all commodities: this element is the socially necessary labour-time which a given commodity embodies.

The labour embodied in the commodity also has a double character: on the one hand, it is defined as *concrete* labour – the outcome of a particular kind of labour – which produces use-value; and on the other hand, as *abstract* labour – the general outcome of the exertion of human effort – which produces exchange value.

So only *abstract* labour is quantitatively comparable. On the capitalist market, commodities are thus compared with respect to the quantity of abstract labour-time they embody. Equivalence between commodities stems from the equivalence between the labour-times socially necessary for their production. 'Just as

12. K. Horney, *La Personnalité névrotique de notre temps*, l'Arche, Paris, 1953, p. 127.

motion', says Marx, 'is measured by time, so is labour by *labour-time*.'[13]

Competition in sport is the comparison of a number of different performances which have an identical element in common, that is to say, a given type of physical effort.

Competition in sport can thus be seen as the institutional framework which enables the comparison of physical activities of the same type: activities which embody different degrees of the same *'value'*. The sports system emerges as the comparison of objective, quantifiable performances which are in principle capable of constant improvement.

In other words, competition involves the idea of *a scale of sporting values,* all of which synthesise to varying degrees a given fraction of the general equivalent.

We can thus treat different performances in sport, or sports 'products', as the specific results of an *abstract 'sports-power'* which involves expending abstract sporting effort. This analysis brings out a constitutive principle of capitalist society, that is to say *the principle of structural comparison.* As L. Sebag writes:

'A commodity producing society develops universal tools of equivalence, evaluation, and accounting. Economic calculation makes it possible to equalise the diversity of products, firms and men, and opens the way to a complete homogenisation of the objects, signs and symbols which structure human existence.'[14]

In conclusion, the sports production process concentrates all the capitalist categories in a specific, original form. *Sport is the political economy of the body as producer.* As such, it has the same status and the same function as the economic categories, which, as Marx said, 'are only the theoretical expressions, the abstractions of the social relations of production'.[15]

13. K. Marx, *Critique of Political Economy,* Lawrence & Wishart, London, 1971, p. 30.
14. L. Sebag, *Marxisme et structuralisme,* Payot, Paris, 1964, p. 66.
15. K. Marx, *The Poverty of Philosophy,* in K. Marx/F. Engels *Collected Works,* Vol. 6, Lawrence & Wishart, London, 1975, p. 165.
    As a set of practical categories, modern sport is bourgeois (or capitalist) in as much as it is the *product* of the capitalist mode of production. For, as Marx explained: 'They (the categories of bourgeois economics) are forms of thought which are socially valid, and therefore objective, for the relations of production belonging to this historically determined mode of social production ie commodity production.' K. Marx, *Capital* Vol. I, Penguin Books, London, 1976, p. 169.

(ii) *Productivity*

Today, productivity is a basic element of industrial social consciousness. For example, as Rigauer points out: 'The structural link between competitive sport and competitive capitalist society is precisely embodied in the principle of productivity: the comparison of performances. Competitive sport is a product of industrial society: a concentrated, symbolic model of its basic principles.'[16]

All the other categories of sport are derived from this category of productivity, central to the capitalist mode of production. We can agree with P. Laguillaumie in saying that 'the schema: competition – productivity – measurement – record is an exact reflection of the process of capitalist production'.[17] Or, as von Krokow notes: 'What makes sport so symbolic is the exactitude, the ideal way in which it promotes the fundamental principles of capitalist society.'[18]

Sport could be described as *the political economy of productivity*.

To say that sport embodies the capitalist principle of productivity implies, as B. Rigauer says, that 'the principle of productivity developed historically on the basis of capitalist industrial production, that is on the basis of the search for the maximisation of profit, along with the accompanying socio-cultural and sociopolitical values and normative rules'.[19]

(iii) *Time*

Time in sport is the abstract quantity measurable with a stopwatch. Much sport is a perpetual race against the clock: a *perpetuum mobile*. This use of time is a pre-condition for any rational technology of the body.

Sports competition is the comparison of sports times on the performance market, which makes it possible to compare two *person/times*. As Marx puts it so well:

'Competition presupposes that labour has been equalised by the subordination of man to the machine or by the extreme divi-

---

16. B. Rigauer, *Sport und Arbeit,* Suhrkamp Verlag, Frankfurt, 1969, p. 26.
17. P. Laguillaumie, 'Pour une critique fondamentale du sport', in *Partisans, Sport, culture et répression,* Maspéro, Paris, 1972, p. 41.
18. C. von Krockow, 'Der Wetteifer in der industriellen Gesellschaft', in *Der Wetteifer,* W. Limpert Verlag, Frankfurt, 1962, p. 59.
19. B. Rigauer, op. cit., p. 28.

sion of labour; that men are effaced by their labour, that the pendulum of the clock has become as accurate a measure of the relative activity of two workers as it is of the speed of two locomotives. Therefore, we should not say that one man's hour is worth another man's hour but rather that one man during an hour is worth just as much as another man during an hour. Time is everything, man is nothing; he is, at most, time's carcase.'[20]

(iv) Space

The reduction of space to geometry, the abstraction of what is concrete, real and tangible in nature, is carried to the ultimate extreme in sport. As A. Ziemilski notes: 'The ideal situation in sport is only achieved when grass, which has already been reduced to its geometrical properties and so to speak artificialised, is actually abandoned for synthetic materials and the race-track thereby loses all connexion with the earth.'[21]

Sport involves a reified way of conceiving the spatial universe.

Spectator sports pour alienated crowds into the industrial craters of the stadiums. L. Mumford accurately notes that 'The stadium becomes a sort of industrial establishment producing running, jumping or football-playing machines'.[22] This reduction of nature to geometry is the root cause of *the removal of play from sport* (*déludisation*): sporting activity is carried out like a factory production process.

Sport is a show-piece of the political economy of the body, which underpins all monopolistic bourgeois forms of physical activity. It serves as a brake on all the demands of the 'Eros-body' for erotic, playful or aesthetic pleasure; demands which could be satisfied through present-day automation under a socialist régime of workers' councils.

(b) Sport and Ideology

The sports system is a text-book example of bureaucracy. The historical development of this system involved the growth of a complex administrative network with its own rules, justice, laws and

20. K. Marx, *The Poverty of Philosophy*, in K. Marx/F. Engels *Collected Works*, Vol. 6, Lawrence & Wishart, London, 1975, p. 127.
21. A. Ziemilski, 'Scepticisme au siècle du sport', in *Recherches internationales à la lumière du marxisme*, No. 48, 1965, p. 9.
22. L. Mumford, *Technics and civilisation*, G. Routledge and Sons, London, 1934.

bureaucrats. To quote W. Tröger:

'Sport has its own laws which influence its forms of organisation. However sport resorts to principles which have long been
adopted by other social groups, and has now developed fully
bureaucratic principles of administration. Present-day sports administration abounds in archives, files, accounts, balance-sheets
and administrative rules.'[23]

This bureaucratic apparatus acquires more and more autonomy
until it becomes a grotesque excrescence on sport. As Tröger
observes:

'As the number of participants increases, the possibilities for
free unorganised sporting activity diminish. . . . As people's lives
are increasingly tied up in the complexities of the industrial age,
and as the drive for high performance demands more and more
time and energy, so practising sportsmen and women are less and
less able to concern themselves with the organisational conditions of their sporting activity. This consequently gives rise to a
body of officials who in the course of time come to constitute an
apparatus, which at the same time gives sport a considerable
weight in the economy.'[24]

Sport has become 'a new form of control', to use Marcuse's
expression. Present-day sports technology helps the bourgeoisie
to establish new forms of repressive control. The Gaullist sports
doctrine openly admits this objective:

'Sport, through the discipline which it requires, brings home the
necessity of order and the benefits of voluntary, organised effort.
The team activity often involved in sport develops a respect for
the loyally established hierarchy, a sense of equality, solidarity
and interdependence. Sport is undoubtedly an excellent
apprenticeship for human relationships: a remarkable school of
sociability.'[25]

In other words, sport trains people to respect the fetishised
state, the national flag, the hierarchy of the factory/barracks or

---

23. W. Tröger, 'Die Organisation des deutschen Sports', in *Das Grosse
    Spiel*, op. cit., p. 47.
24. *Ibidem*, p. 49.
25. *Essai de doctrine du sport*, Haut Comité des Sports, Paris, 1965, p. 22.

the school/prison.

Finally it is important to indicate the role of spectator sports in *reducing the population to a mass with a potentially fascist dynamic.*

3.　The Functions of the Institution of Sport

These observations on the phenomenon of sport enable us to look briefly at its socio-political and ideological functions.

(a)　Sport and Capitalism

To summarise:

(i)　Sport is a new sector in the capitalist production process, within the capitalist division of labour. Sport creates surplus value from the production of commodities such as foot-wear, balls, skis, tourism, sports equipment etc.

(ii)　Sport is an advertising medium: sportsmen are turned into sandwich-board men.

(iii)　Sport helps to improve the industrial output of the economy by increasing the productivity of the worker.

(iv)　Sport promotes the economic development and tourist industry of entire regions, such as Grenoble or Munich.

(v)　Sport constitutes a profitable sector of the capitalist entertainments industry: sport is sold as a commodity on a competitive market. Sports enterprises such as clubs come within capitalist social relations of production.

(b)　The Political functions of sport

(i)　*By promoting identification with its champions, sport subtly inculcates attachment to the established order.* As such sport has a function of stabilising the present system.

(ii)　Sport is an *opiate of the people,* turning the masses away from the socialist revolution and the class struggle: the function of diversion.

(iii)　Sport is a means of *regimenting youth* (amply exploited by Hitler, Mussolini, Pétain, Franco and de Gaulle).

(iv)　*Sport promotes class-collaboration,* both within the enterprise in the form of Company sport, and in society as a whole by its pretention to political 'neutrality', by encouraging a reasonable dialogue between 'both sides of industry' who play the game according to a sort of 'sporting social contract' governed by an 'impartial referee' – the bourgeois state.

(v)   Sport is supposed to be an example of *peaceful coexistence* between 'states with different social systems' and thus serves to back up this counter-revolutionary policy.

(vi)   Sport assists the powers that be to promote chauvinism, racism, nationalism and xenophobia among the masses.

(vii)   Sport is a powerful factor in the militarisation of society and the preparation for imperialist war – everyone knows how highly the army values sport. . . .

(c)   The ideological functions of sport

(i)   Sport is an ideologocial State apparatus which fulfils a triple role: it ideologically reproduces bourgeois social relations such as selection and hierarchy, subservience, obedience etc.; secondly, it spreads an organisational ideology specific to the institution of sport, involving competition, records and output; and thirdly, it transmits on a huge scale the general themes of ruling bourgeois ideology like the myth of the superman, individualism, social advancement, success, efficiency etc.

(ii)   Sport is an ideological crystallisation of permanent competition, which is presented as 'preparation for the struggle for life'.

(iii)   Sport is an ideology based on the myth of indefinite, linear progress, as expressed in the upward curve of sports records.

(iv)   Finally, sport is the *ideology of the body/machine* – the body turned into a robot, alienated by capitalist labour. Sport is based on *the fantasy of the 'fit', productive body*.

(d)   Sport's function is repressive socialisation

Competitive sport at school is a repressive and alienating form of education, adapted to the interests of the bourgeoisie. It is no accident that J. Comiti wanted to 'bring competitive sport into schools on a big scale'.

(i)   School and university sport is the *mass base for recruitment* to top-level sport outside.

(ii)   School sport trains the child for his or her future as an exploited wage-slave in the labour market.

(iii)   Sport is a systematic form of sexual repression which de-eroticises the body and cultivates sado-masochism. It imposes a sport-like, genital sexuality – sexual gymnastics – which fits in with the norms of bourgeois monogamy.

(iv)   Sport develops a standardised social image of the body which tends to deform the way adolescents relate to their own bodies.

(v)   Finally, sport is a 'character school' which aims at creating authoritarian, narcissistic, aggressive and obedient personality structures. 'Sport is a powerful ally of morality', as M. Herzog wrote some years ago . . .

(e)   The functions of sport as mythology

(i)   The huge success of sport is based on the fact that it embodies certain prevalent myths. Sport is a living, dramatic *mythology*. The most important of these myths are structured around three re-current themes:

– Who is the strongest man, the fastest sprinter, the highest jumper alive today?

– Who was the first man in history to run a 10 second 100 metres, to clear 2.20 metres in the high-jump etc.? – the 'magic barriers'.

– Finally, who can match up to the 'sporting' performance of animals? – the idea of imaginary contests between different species.

These themes can be related to the œdipal myth of the 'Hero' who overcomes his father or sleeps with his mother – the exploit of the first to make love with her.

(ii)   Sport is a system of obsessive, repetitive and hence ritual-ised ceremonies, dominated by proto-fascist and militaristic rites: military music, medal ceremonies, rhythmic marches, Nuremburg-style rallies etc.

Conclusion

This article lays no claim to be comprehensive or definitive. Its aim is simply *to open up a discussion on sport*.

The *Ecole Emancipée* is working on the development of alterna-tive, non-alienating and non-repressive forms of physical education.

J.-M. Brohm and Bernard Yanez. May 1974.

The Sports Mode of Production: East Germany*

The German Democratic Republic was set up just after the Second World War while the country was occupied by the tanks of the Soviet Army. Since then this state has constantly claimed to be building 'scientific socialism'. Our present aim is not to assess the socio-economic successes and failures of this attempt. We are instead trying to show the link between the 'building of socialism' and the establishment of a sports apparatus with an astonishing productivity, which has placed this small country among the top sporting nations.

In East Germany after the War, the establishment of a productive apparatus based on heavy industry entailed the scientific organisation of work and in particular, biological rationalisation of the labour-power of the workers. That is the general basis for the massive, intensive and universal practice of competitive sport in the country of 'socialism in one country'. Sport was an indispensable means for establishing *bureaucratic State-capitalism in E. Germany*. As a prioritised branch of the bureaucratic state apparatus, sport itself has become *bureaucratic, State-sport: cybernetic sport*. The building of state capitalism in E. Germany required a skilled and tough work-force, which explains the importance attached to the state sports system as a means of producing working sportsmen and sporting workers. E. Germany resembles a vast, 'democratic' concentration camp, cut off by the Berlin wall, that symbol of so-called 'socialist' freedom in the East. A look at the sports system brings to mind a sports factory or a sports barracks: sport has become an essential productive force. Such a penetration of competitive sport into all spheres of society has

*First published by Christian Bourgois, Paris, 1976 in *Critiques du Sport*.

turned E. Germany into a vast sports laboratory or sports enterprise – some would go as far as to say a sports prison.

At the superstructural or political level, the obligation to take
part in sport is written into the E. German constitution. In Article
18 of this 'socialist' constitution we read: 'Physical education
and sport are elements of the culture of all citizens, contributing
to their physical and intellectual development.' Article 26: 'Art,
Culture, Sport and Tourism are integral parts of the scientific and
technical revolution and contribute to the development of the
personality.' Article 34: 'Every citizen has a right to physical
education and sport.' A declaration of principle by the State
Council of September 20th, 1968, is still more explicit: 'In the
German Democratic Republic, the programme of socialism corresponds to the interests of the workers and the youth. This makes it
possible to satisfy their desire to practice physical education and
sport in a new, socialist (sic) way, for the benefit of the people
as a whole.'[1]

The late Walter Ulbricht recently stated (1970): 'Every citizen
who today practices a sport actively and regularly is acting wise-
ly, both in his own interest and in the interest of his family and
of society as a whole. To devote time to the practice of sport
is to devote time to your own health and well-being, to your intellectual and physical adaptability and to your ability to do well at
school, at work and in your personal and social life.'[2]

State sport is strongly *recommended*, or in other words, compulsory. It is thus a key element in the building of bureaucratic
state capitalism, referred to as 'socialism'. 'Socialist' sport is one of
the ways people are enthusiastically trained for work – sport is
work – and above all, it is a way of indoctrinating people to
serve the 'socialist state' and the single 'workers'' party. In E.
Germany sport is an important means of diverting the exploited
masses from politics through military-style state organisation.
'Marxist-Leninist' sport is subservient to a 'statist' ideology of mass
regimentation. 'Party spirit' in E. German 'socialist' sport means
the training of citizens for production and for devotion to and
defence of the 'socialist fatherland'. Official Party instructions
specify that the organisation of sport is the responsibility of all

---

1. Quoted by R. Passevant in *les Mystères du sport en RDA*, les Editeurs
   français, Paris, 1973, p. 164.
2. Ibidem, p. 165.

state bodies – unions, cooperatives, the army, youth organisations, etc.: 'The organisation of an advanced socialist social system requires the development of socialist physical education,
through the participation of all state bodies and social organisations, all of which have a responsibility in the field of physical
education and sport.'[3]

So what does 'marxist-leninist' sport look like? The E. German
sports system, which is regarded as the model for all the countries
of Eastern Europe, has three tasks: firstly, to inculcate 'socialist
class-consciousness' in the population through the politicisation of
sport; to develop the physical and mental qualities needed to train
a work-force of 'socialist' workers; and finally to inculcate the
moral and ideological principles of the new, scientific conception
of life under socialism. So sport provides physical, moral and
intellectual training.

1. The pervading presence of sport in all institutions: the State sport monolith

At the top of the State sports system in E. Germany are three
organisations:
– the Ministry for Culture,
– the DTSB (*Deutscher Turn und Sport Bund*). This German sport
and gymnastics confederation brings the equivalent of national
federations for particular sports under one coordinating body.
While it is not formally speaking a State body, all its officials and
its material and financial resources come from the State.
– The Ministry for Youth and Popular Education.

There is also a 'Committee for physical education and sport',
which has the job of passing down governmental instructions to
the Ministry for Culture, the DTSB and the Ministry for Youth and
Popular Education, and of coordinating the activities of these para-
state bodies. This coordination is carried out at all levels of the
system, through regular meetings between officials of the different
organisations. The DTSB is a federation of all the sports clubs
which are represented on it by 'elected' delegates. At the base, these
'elected' delegates of the clubs form local DTSB committees. Above
these there are regional committees, corresponding roughly to re-

3. Ibidem, p. 86.

gional leagues in France, which are organised by a regional management. And the national management of the DTSB is in turn linked to the Committee for Physical Education and Sport. The administration of the DTSB is in the hands of state-paid officials but the day-to-day running of the organisation is carried out by the representatives of the clubs. This civilian sports institution is closely tied in with other state apparatuses: the army, the police, the party, youth associations, enterprises, unions, cooperatives etc. As a French communist, Y. Adam puts it: *'Sport pervades every institution.'*[4]

In fact the horizontal criss-crossing of the institutions of sport makes it a state monolith: sport forms a sort of connective tissue between the various organisations of the country. This monolith makes E. Germany comparable to a kind of huge all-sports club where every worker is a sportsman and every sportsman a worker, under the aegis of the 'Watchman/State' and the 'Guiding Party, the Great Marxist-Leninist Teacher.' In this situation sport is a realisation of the Platonic dream of generalised control through indoctrination starting in early childhood. E. Germany is like a vast racing-stables or sports-barracks turning out champions to represent 'socialism' abroad. In this small country of 18 million inhabitants, 70 to 80 per cent of the population belong to sports clubs and 20 per cent of all adults regularly practice a competitive sport with regular training and periodic competitions. For the others, the DTSB has set up a special organisation to run sports events which, in 1971, were attended by three million people . . . In short, *sport in E. Germany is a truly mass activity, controlled by the Party and the State.* In 1969, E. Germany had 31,500 sports centres, as against 28,500 in 1968. These included 350 stadiums, 650 swimming pools, more than 800 sports fields and nearly 7,000 specialised training and games centres. In 1968, 2,380,000 young people took part in the Children's and Young People's Games: the 'Spartaciad'. The DTSB has two million members of whom 300,000 are between 14 and 18 years old: that represents 28.8 per cent of the age-group. Needless to say, this institutional infrastructure is tightly supervised through a systematic, administrative control network. E. Germany is split up into 217 regions or 'Kreise' and the sporting life of the country is structured by this organisational spider's web. *The sports structure is at its*

4. *Le Monde* of 25.11.71.

strongest at the enterprise and factory level. Thus, apart from a few big clubs – such as Dynamo of Berlin – which are all-sports clubs open to the public and to students, most sports clubs in E. Germany are 'Enterprise Sports Communities' (*Bethiebssports-gemeinschaften*) and people are systematically directed towards these enterprise clubs when they leave school. The country is also covered by a network of trainers, youth leaders and physical education teachers who contribute to the selection and training of the élite.

2. Sport at School

School, where sport is compulsory, is the place where the athletes 'who bring in the medals' are raised, according to an E. German sports official.[5] The universal and compulsory practice of sport at school, starting from the earliest age, is what explains the huge productivity of the 'socialist' sports mode of production. 'It all starts at school,' write F. Rousseau and G. Sandoz in *le Nouvel Observateur*. 'Two to four hours compulsory sport a week for all, and that means real sport, not the pathetic routine seen in French schools. Bad marks for physical education are enough to fail an exam. There are swimming pools, stadiums and gymnasiums everywhere.'[6]

Propaganda encourages children and adolescents to practice sport for the good of the 'socialist state'. An early introduction to sport is recommended, starting in the lowest class (six to seven year-olds), based on a limited range of five or six sports; from the age of ten to 13 the programme comprises 40 per cent sports training in two sports, 40 per cent complementary physical education and 20 per cent swimming as a third sport; from the age of 13 to 17 it comprises 70 per cent training in two sports and 30 per cent general physical education. As Y. Adam stresses: 'The generalisation of sports teaching at school from the earliest age brings out preferences and aptitudes and poses the problem of finding the forms through which young talents can best express themselves, in conjunction with the level reached by world sport: in E. Germany, young people specialise in sport as they would in

5. *Le Monde* of 20.2.70.
6. *Le Nouvel Observateur* of 3.9.72.

any other aspects of culture.'⁷ Today eight-year-old children can be seen being timed to the tenth of a second and attempting to beat records! What with school, district and provincial championships, more and more competitions are organised for young people. These enable trainers to spot their young hopefuls early. What better example of the ideal of immersing youth in sport.

Every two years since 1966, a 'Spartaciad' has been held. The torch for these children's games is lit at Buchenwald near a plaque commemorating the death there of Ernst Thälmann, the German communist leader. It is carried in procession to Berlin. The young athletes take an oath: they swear to strive to win 'for the honour of the German Democratic Republic and for the glory of sport, in the spirit of socialism, peace and friendship'. In 1970 more than three million school children aged betwen seven and 18 took part in the qualifying competitions. The ten thousand finalists were brought together in a sort of Olympic village in Berlin. Twenty-four events were represented.

Thus permanent competition for young people is institutionalised according to age and ability. After passing through the various stages of this selection process, young sportsmen and women may achieve the rank of champions. A 'sports badge' is given to children who reach a certain level of performance, fixed for their age-group. In other words, young E. Germans learn at an early age the identity between the productivity principle and the principles of E. German monopoly state-capitalism.

For particularly talented students, E. Germany has special centres which serve as the nursery-beds or the factories for the production of future 'socialist champions'. In these hot-house conditions are bred the colts and fillies to be paraded in the stadiums for the glory of 'socialism', sport, peace and 'freedom'. The mass production of little E. German sports machines is further refined through sports training centres. Thus, in addition to the 'circles' and clubs which surround every educational institution, and in addition to the enterprise, union and military clubs and the innumerable sports associations which cover the whole country, there are special ten-year schools (sic) which specialise in just a few disciplines. Children go to these centres at the age of ten – the fifth class – on the basis of a decision taken jointly by the family, the head of the child's previous school and the specialised

7. *Le Monde* of 25.11.71 (our emphasis).

physical education teacher. Moreover, specialisation exists even within the framework of ordinary school life, in the form of 'training groups'. According to Y. Adam, 'These are made up of young people who remain members of their original sporting community – school, factory or district – but who come together two or three times a week for training. These young people also follow one or two three-week training courses during the school holidays. The advanced training centre is generally sited near a club which provides the right material conditions.'[8] As can be seen, the sports network is everywhere, organising sports activity in schools so as to channel the best pupils towards the clubs and top-level competition. It is a systematic application of the 'fish-pond' theory – the tiddlers bred in the pond are fished out to restock the sports system.

But E. German sports theoreticians, driven by their obsessive preoccupation with sporting productivity, have pushed the search for future champions even further. It now starts at the nursery school. A confidential document emanating from the Leipzig research institute and quoted by *Spiegel*, entitled 'The organisational structures and operation of training centres', states: 'Preparation for the Olympic Games must start before school-age. If we can convince crêche and nursery school teachers of this, it should be possible to analyse the development of the child over at least the three years before he goes to school and thereby obtain the information needed to improve his sports education.'[9] This Stalinist, cybernetic and technocratic conception has been taken to the point where it has even been thought acceptable to hold a sports file on every child. It has always been an ambition of totalitarian régimes to get the whole population on file. It is close to being achieved in E. Germany. Thus a national sports card has actually been established, which records the body measurements, the results of medical examinations and the successive performances of each individual. 'It is essential to start selection very early, in the first or second year at school,' states a report to sports inspectors, *'otherwise there is a danger that children will become interested in subjects or get into circles that have nothing to do with sport.'*[10] This quotation is very important, in that it admits to the falsity of

8. *Le Monde* of 25.11.71.
9. Quoted in *Le Nouvel Observateur* of 3.9.72.
10. Ibidem.

the claim that children *naturally* experience a need for competitive sport. Despite official denials, competitive sport is in fact imposed on them from a very early age by the E. German sports apparatus, with the aim of turning them into sports robots. What does this quotation really say? It says that children spontaneously become interested in things other than competitive sport (*not* to be confused with playful, collective, free physical activity), unless they are forced to become involved in the E. German state sports machinery. It is interesting to note that this so-called 'natural need' for competitive sport is pre-supposed in the same terms by the Gaullist sports doctrine, which incidentally expresses great admiration for the E. German sports system. The document states that 'Sport is thus an *imposed discipline* (for adolescents) but it *should* (sic) also be one of their favourite leisure pursuits. That is its specific character'.[11] This contradiction between discipline and free choice sums up all the cultural and ideological contradictions of sports technology, which is quite aware that sports training and competition are not natural needs in children, experienced as a vocation, but are constraints and obligations imposed, particularly in E. Germany, by the coercive methods of the bureaucratic police apparatus and by ideological pressure. (The article from *Le Nouvel Observateur*, quoted above, cites a number of instructive examples of how sportsmen and women are constrained to accept 'freely' the sports discipline of the party and the state.)

This 'Asiatic' sports mode of production in which the Moloch of the state rules supreme, is founded on a *veritable trust* or combine. From the age of seven the child is taken in charge by institutions of control and progressively directed towards generalised sporting competition: Plato's dream come true. The state itself becomes a sort of club, specialised in the mass production of 'socialist' state champions, who are docile and loyal to the régime. In short, *E. Germany cultivates a sporting conception of the state and a state conception of sport*. All citizens are potential competitors. The population is educated in a sporting spirit by the teacher-state which takes on the appearance of a vast federation of factory, army and union clubs. The entire social formation of E. Germany is covered by sports facilities. E. Germany is a vast sports

11. *Essai de doctrine du sport*, Haut Comité des sports, Paris, 1965, p. 31 (our emphasis).

factory: a sports super-enterprise. The social and political role of mass and élite sport in E. Germany is clearly laid down. Through their performance at work, in their studies and in the stadiums, sportsmen and women must contribute to the strengthening of the Democratic Republic. Through the force of their example they must encourage the practice of sport among young people. They thereby contribute to the reproduction of the institution of sport itself, by guaranteeing an adequate field of recruitment. Within the context of Stakhanovism in industry and 'socialist' emulation in sport, the state seeks to organise the maximum number of people in a series of interlinked apparatuses: sport, the army, industry, the unions, youth associations etc. As an E. German newspaper writes: 'In sport we can never rest on our laurels. The constant betterment of records is the proof of this. Every evening after work and at the weekend everyone must strive after new re-cords.'[12] M. Castaing adds the rather ironic comment: 'It must be said that this striving after "the inhuman work pace," when the object is supposed to be relaxation and joy, can only be described as a form of Stakhanovism.'[13]

Jean-Marie Brohm. June 1964.

12. Quoted in *Le Monde* of 20.2.70 (our emphasis).
13. *Le Monde* of 20.2.70.

The Significance of Physical Leisure in The 'Leisure Civilisation'*

Today's exhausting and stifling living conditions, the mutilation of the organism through labour, and the generalised physiological irritation caused by 'technicist civilisation' necessitate the large scale organisation of *generalised physical compensation* if the individual is to be able to go on living and functioning in this hostile environment. Exhaustion, tension, listlessness, in short, the generalisation of muscular and especially nervous fatigue make recuperation techniques a necessity for the stability of the system. Moreover, the many deep physical frustrations involved in work and city life in the capitalist system can only be forgotten about and neutralised by a certain amount of 'libidinal' satisfaction, physical gratification and pleasure. That is the main function of techniques for relaxation, escapism and physical ecstasy which are increasingly proliferating.

The very development of capitalist society has thus produced forms of physical leisure pursuit and types of bodily activity whose functions are precisely determined by the system. The 'bodily techniques', to use Mauss's famous expression, employed in leisure pursuits are essentially techniques on the one hand for recuperation and on the other hand, for getting away from it all, for escapism and ecstasy.

There are at least two fundamental reasons why 'bodily leisure activities' have become a necessity for the present system.

Firstly, *from an economic point of view*, the present level of industrialisation and urbanisation under capitalist régimes or 'peoples democracies' requires physical activities for readjustment and compensation. The daily assaults on the organism by today's

---

*First appeared in *Partisans*, Sport, culture et répression, op. cit.

industrial, urban environment are a threat to health. The rhythm and pace of work in industry, and working hours and schedules determined solely by the profitability of the production apparatus destroy traditional biological rhythms, since the organism is required to be capable of production at any time. Night-work, the three shift system etc. mean that the basic functioning of the organism has to be geared to the productive apparatus. Marx's statement has never been more true: 'The individual is a mere appendage of the machine.'[1] The organism itself is mechanised. Work becomes more and more exacting, requiring an increasingly sustained effort. Mechanised and atomised industrial working conditions, machine-watching jobs needing constant attention, and the working conditions in work-shops, offices, factories, construction sites etc. require a greater and greater mobilisation of the organism. The result is considerable nervous and physical fatigue.

Fatigue due to working conditions is not all that people have to put up with. They also have to withstand urban living conditions. Under capitalism the city is like a concentration camp, with its overcrowding, air pollution, shortage of open spaces, dehumanising public transport, perpertual, massive noise, the terroristic assault from advertising, the density of housing, sickening smells etc. This environment too does serious and permanent damage to the organism. The organism is increasingly subject to intolerable tensions in hostile surroundings which brutalise it and grind it down. So physical activities have to be found, not just to compensate for these assaults, but also to train the organism to withstand them better. That is the essential task of the two main kinds of recuperation techniques: *compensatory physical activities* to 'repair' the organism and physical activities for adjustment to 'prepare' it. Such recuperation techniques are calculated to maintain the profitability of labour power.

Secondly, *from a political point of view*, distractions, physical relaxation and getting away from it all are first and foremost ideological ways of running away from reality: they are techniques of escapism. It is in the interests of the system to promote

1. As K. Marx makes clear in *Capital* Vol. I, Penguin Books, London 1976: 'Man, deprived of leisure, whose whole life is punctuated by the sole physical necessity of sleeping, eating etc. . . . , whose whole life is consumed by work in the service of a capitalist, that man is lowlier than a beast of burden. He is a mere machine for producing alien wealth; dulled in mind and broken in body.'

physical leisure activities in order to preserve the individual's capacity for work. But it is equally important for the system to prevent the content of these activities taking on any form other than a physical one. The most reactionary political régimes have always seen open-air physical leisure pursuits and activities as an excellent outlet. Scouting, an extreme form of this ideological dehumanisation, is a perfect example of the outlawing of any critical ways of thinking. *Muscular activity is a good substitute for critical, mental activity.* Then again, physical escapism gives a psychic shot in the arm, a dose of optimism, a means of looking at life through rose-tinted spectacles. It is not surprising to find that conservative or reactionary forces have always preached sport as an alternative to politics. The extension of physical leisure activities implies the phenomenon of the de-politicisation of youth. It is not surprising either to find that the PCF, as it has taken a more and more counter-revolutionary course, has attempted to keep its youth movements happy by offering them a return to leisure activities and sport. Physical leisure activities in fact constitute the best way of dulling and intellectually neutralising the masses.

Let us look at some of the features of this physical leisure civilisation.

The Technocrats of Physical Recuperation

Present day civilisation is giving rise on a large scale to the emergence of individuals and organisations whose jobs or functions are in one way or another concerned with the administration or organisation of physical activity. These are the *technocrats of the body*: the 'maintenance and repair men' of the human organism. There are many different types of such technocrats, but they all have the same functions: to tone up, heal, repair, train and shape the body so that it can operate adequately in 'technicist' civilisation.[2]

First of all, at the top of the ladder, there are the de-luxe technocrats whose job is to recondition the tired old hides of the bourgeoisie and its lackeys. They are expected to make new from old, to patch up and conserve what is worn out and faded. A whole industry has developed around this 'physical renovation', with spe-

2. Cf. The ideology behind 'keep fit!'

cialised centres bringing together all the necessary services,[3] where tired and embittered company directors can relax by taking thermal cures seasoned with sauna baths and massages. These worthy citizens can enjoy the benefits of ray-treatment centres, water cures, sea-air cures etc. As for intellectuals, they go in for relaxation courses, yoga and buddhist or other forms of self-mastery, while dynamic engineers and managers practice judo, physical training, body culture and psycho-physical recuperation in specialised gymnasiums. Thus the upper crust get their lost energies back by paying technocrats to restore their physical fitness, their dynamism and well-being. Masseurs, physical training instructors, physiotherapists, judo instructors, chiropodists, manicurists and physical technocrats of every shape and form all sell their different wares under the label: physical fitness and well-being.[4]

At a more 'democratic' level, the masses (or at least those who possess a radio set), have the right to benefit freely from 'early morning exercises'. First thing every morning the voice of a physical persuasion expert, set to music, encourages them to get into shape for the day. The right mood and physical fitness are preconditions for a good day's work. This psycho-muscular preparation is one of many aspects of the early morning mobilisation for work which runs right through all fields of mass culture. Starting the day right, through this kind of warming up procedure, even if it is not practised on a mass scale, typifies the technocracy of the future: *specialised dispensaries of fitness (in every sense of the word) for work*. In the army, the not inappropriate names for this magnificent muscular exercise vary from one unit to another: 'Early morning clean-up'; 'Wake up with a flourish'; 'Shaking the rust off'; 'Starting the day right'.

But things get more serious when the technocrats take it on themselves to bring relief to the workers at their place of work, seeking to facilitate their task in the name of humanitarianism. At that point the 'leisure technicians' become direct agents of class exploitation. Recuperation instructors are then directly fulfilling the role of consultants in Stakhanovism. Many experiments have been carried out in this field both in the East and the West,

---

3. In *le Corps dans la vie quotidienne*, Epi, Paris, 1974, p. 15, A. Danilo and P. Stevenin speak of 'Service Stations for the body'!
4. See also the relevant exposure of this ideology by J. Baudrillard in *La Société de consommation*, 'Idées', Gallimard, Paris, 1970.

with the aim of rationalising the organisation of recuperation. Breaks for physical jerks, physical recuperation sessions at the work place, periods for individual or collective relaxation, often accompanied by music, intensive physical education for young workers etc. – all these techniques of physical mobilisation directly under the auspices of the company are being increasingly developed, systematised and rationalised. But the basic objective is always the same: to manipulate labour power so as to extract the maximum absolute or relative surplus value; to integrate the work force as much as possible into the company as its 'natural environment'; to increase output and to train workers to be able to overcome fatigue and sublimate their drives in productive effort.

This kind of physical technocracy has become a necessity for a society based on class exploitation. As the rationalisation of production becomes more and more repressive and the worker is increasingly just a cog in the machine, manipulated by either the owners of the means of production or bureaucratic 'leaders', so leisure activity and 'rest' time in the enterprise tend to function as the *physical rationalisation of labour power*. In the countries of the Eastern Bloc, where the Stakhanovite tradition is strongly established, experiments of this kind have been rapidly systematised on a mass scale. Their sole purpose is to tie the worker down to his enterprise and to enable him to find joy in the production of the greatest possible output,[5] to teach him to toil away without wavering and to develop qualities of discipline, will-power and strength. From an economic point of view, from the moment the individual is conceived of as a mere productive force to be exploited, exercises at work are no more than a technique for manipulating the work force under the control, needless to say, of the management. 'In every case of structured forms of physical education, the exercises should be carried out under the enlightened guidance of an official', concludes a physical education bureaucrat in a study of *'Physical education and work in socialist society'*.[6]

The contemporary capitalist state has not been slow to grasp the benefits to be gained from employing such a profession of

5. Recall the sinister Nazi slogans: 'Kraft durch Freude', and 'Arbeit macht frei' ('strength through joy' and 'work makes you free').
6. *Recherches internationales à la lumière du marxisme, Sport et éducation physique*, Editions de la Nouvelle Critique, No. 48, June/July 1965, p. 117.

enlightened recuperation technicians.

'It is obviously in everybody's interest to promote greater well-being, to facilitate work and reduce the nervous strain on the workers and thereby *contribute to the improvement of human relationships between members of the enterprise* as well as helping to improve the prevention of industrial accidents.'[7]

Thus *another form of fatigue* is being proposed as necessary therapy to compensate for the fatigue of the factory or office. This exercise must obviously be closely controlled.

'All enterprises *should be obliged* . . . to take on a member of staff to be responsible for the physical training of the work-force. . . . These instructors should be qualified in *leisure techniques*. . . . They should have everyone's confidence so that they can organise, manage and initiate activity. They should take their place within the company hierarchy with management status and enjoy normal career prospects.'[8]

Although this para-police type of education has not yet been systematically put into practice, its political implications are strikingly clear. The state needs physical education managers within the enterprises themselves to maintain output and ensure adequate 'human' conditions for exploiting labour. The traditional foreman could well be replaced in future by a physical education instructor. Breaks for physical jerks would then become a direct means of class exploitation. Their true purpose is to integrate the worker joyfully into the enterprise, to adjust him totally to his job so that work becomes the sole content of his life. The French government's 1966 *White Paper on Youth* comments:

'Several successful experiments prove that in work situations a judicious use of physical and sporting activity enables workers to adapt themselves to their jobs, helps to prevent accidents, *improves the climate of labour relations and reduces absenteeism*: breaks for physical jerks lead to a beneficial easing of tension.'[9]

7. *Essai de doctrine du sport,* Haut Comité des Sports, Paris, 1965, p. 59 (our emphasis).
8. Ibid, p. 62 (our emphasis).
9. *Livre Blanc de la Jeunesse,* Paris, 1966, p. 368 (our emphasis).

Physical leisure activities and relaxation: the psychic shot in the arm

We have just briefly looked at how labour technocrats manage 'adjustment activities', to use J. Dumazedier's term, or in other words, adaptation to alienated labour. This adjustment is really that of labour power, conceived in its most totally reified abstraction: as the pure source of surplus value obedient to the demands of productivity. But physical adaptation to 'industrial, technicist civilisation' has to be compensated for by activities which can repair the resulting damage to the organism. This is the particular thesis of J. Dumazedier's article in which he explains his conception of individual leisure in the field of physical education.[10] He argues that for leisure pursuits to fulfil their function, physical and sports education must have a special place.

> 'If physical education is treated as an aspect of leisure, it will become first and foremost an activity implying rest, the removal of tension and tiredness, almost going as far as relaxation. Such activity is increasingly necessary in surroundings full of noise, agitation, tensions and preoccupations caused by the concentration of so many human beings and the complexity of our civilisation.'

Dumazedier is perfectly aware of the role to be played by physical and sports education within mass culture. (His positions coincide with those of the official Sports Doctrine.) Such education is a factor of social order and stability, or in short, social peace, in that it dissipates tensions and produces a salutory relaxation. Dumazedier assigns a purely compensatory role to physical leisure pursuits. Periodically the organism needs to relax and get back into shape. Leisure is just a process of recuperation or functional renewal, totally integrated into the bourgeois order: an institution as necessary for the healthy functioning of the system as annual holidays. In other words, Dumazedier seeks to smooth the path of alienated labour, but with means from *outside* the sphere of production. The exploited, brutalised worker has the right to take a breather *after*

10.   J. Dumazedier, *'Education physique, sport et sociologie'*, in *Education physique et sports*, No. 69. Another work by the same author should be mentioned since it was all the rage and became a touchstone for the modernist bourgeoisie: *Vers une civilisation du loisir*, le Seuil, Paris, 1962.

work – to have a game of bowls or go fishing. He will then come back fresh and ready to start work again.

The *Draft Sports Doctrine* fills out Dumazedier's ideas on this question, or rather makes them more precise. 'By enabling the individual, through training, to withstand fatigue better and to increase his efficiency by improving his physical and nervous potential and conserving his youthfulness, sport creates a type of freedom which is too often disregarded: *physical freedom*.'[11] So, for the apostles of capital, physical freedom is equated with the ability to withstand fatigue, to sweat surplus value more profitably, and the readiness to sacrifice one's youth for work. In his own time, Marx already remarked that capital sought ways of lengthening the active life of the wage worker. In physical leisure pursuits and sport, capital seems to have discovered the Fountain of Youth for its wage slaves. Sport lengthens youth, that is to say the productive capacity of the worker and the life of his labour-power. Dumazedier's caricature of leisure fits in entirely with the rationalisation of labour. Marx, unlike Dumazedier, never defined leisure as recuperation, but rather as *free time*. 'Free time – the time available either to enjoy the product or to realise oneself freely – that is true wealth.'[12]

Following from his original definition of leisure as recuperation, Dumazedier outlines a programme of leisure activities for all, that is to say for that part of the population depressed and dulled by labour – leisure for *wage-slaves*. Thus for him, leisure becomes another kind of labour, whereas for Marx, leisure presupposed the abolition of wage-labour, a communist régime and automation. As P. Naville correctly notes:

'Leisure, particularly when practised *en masse* and through the mass media of the stadiums, radio sets and television screens, is orientated towards the recovery of strength and of the minimal

11. *Essai de doctrine du sport*, op. cit., p. 18 (our emphasis).
12. K. Marx, *Theories of Surplus Value, III*, quoted by M. Rubel, *Pages choisies pour une éthique socialiste*, Librairie M. Rivière, Paris, 1948, p. 282: 'Such time will not be taken up with directly productive work but will be set aside for pleasure, and leisure activities, enabling individuals to devote themselves to free activity and self development.'
   Marx expands on this conception of leisure and free time at length in the *Grundrisse*, Penguin Books, London, 1973. On this question the reader should refer to the important work of R. Rosdolsky, *The Genesis of Marx's 'Capital'*, Pluto Press, London, 1977.

stability needed to be able to work well. In any social system ruled by the iron law of labour, whether wage labour or not, periods of relaxation can never be more than time to recuperate for the effort of production. Rest is just the meagre reward for exhaustion and the promise of the next period of tension.'[13]

'Then,' says Dumazedier, 'physical education is a preparation for distraction. Monotony and boredom are growing evils in technicist civilisation. They give rise to an increased need for games. Early training in gymnastic pastimes is an element of stability in our society. The playing field and bowls patch are just as important as stadiums.'

Dumazedier recognises that ever since Roman times games have always had a useful role as a safety valve and diversion. A society that exudes boredom has to be able to provide its members with amusements. Sport will see to that! Physical leisure is thus a means of dulling people intellectually: an opiate. Given this role as a factor of 'stability in society', it is easy to see why education-alists seek to provide idle or unemployed young people with this type of leisure activity. As a true man of the people, Dumazedier sings the praises of the bowls patch, but if it is 'games' he is after, he could just as well hold up the betting shop, the football pools or the card games which make up the greater part of the cultural leisure pursuits of an intellectually impoverished population. Bowls, fishing and gardening are in fact a classic range of hobbies.

What is more, the recommended 'personal life-style', as the Gaullist leisure charter frankly admits, is a 'style' of control and submission to discipline.

'Physical and sports education is one of the directed activities which fills young people's lives *and will continue to do so when they go on to become apprentices or soldiers*. In short, sport, for them, is an imposed discipline, but it should also be one of their favourite leisure pursuits.'[14]

In other words, for young people, sport is held to be a freely imposed leisure pursuit – a voluntarily accepted constraint, par-ticularly when they are under the authority of the boss or army officer!

13. P. Naville, *De l'aliénation à la jouissance*, Librairie M. Rivière, Paris, 1957, p. 489.
14. *Essai de doctrine du sport*, op. cit., p. 31.

The Flight Back to Nature and Tourism

Compensation is provided by the flight back to nature, which is just as controlled and managed. This is the phenomenon of holidays: mass travel, camping, open air leisure pursuits, naturism etc. Within specially laid out enclosures, the individual has the right to recover from the damage done to his organism by the carceral environment of work and city. These leisure zones and 'natural' parks are a caricature of truly free leisure activity and wild nature. Physical compensation is itself carefully controlled and the whole holiday phenomenon is run by the system. *We have already reached the stage where the masses are periodically let out on leave.* At given, prearranged times certain categories of workers are let loose for holidays which have to be taken at that time rather than another.* The mass departures and homecomings are organised on a grand scale by the police so as to ensure that the masses leave and return to work safe and sound. Contemporary mass travel, with the system of annual paid holidays and holiday transport is really a huge migration organisation: the producers are sent off at fixed times of year to get a bit of fresh air, sun and sea on the beaches or by the rivers. However the system is not yet sufficiently rationalised. There is already talk of spreading out the holiday period by sending people off at different times so as to organise holidays in a way which is compatible with the efficient running of the gigantic production system and which above all corresponds to the private interests of the tourist industry.

Physical activities are programmed into the leisure activities controlled by the system. The mushrooming of so many private, public and semi-public holiday organisations is an indication of this. The individual is completely taken in hand and has only to follow the planned or proposed itinerary and time-table. Holiday clubs are just a de-luxe caricature of the same phenomenon. The organisation of holidays is rationalised, pre-planned and timed according to a detailed programme. The return to nature is carried out under administrative control. Official camping sites represent the most 'democratic' but also the most terroristic element

[*This phenomenon, though true to a great extent in all advanced capitalist countries, finds its perfect expression in the French holiday system. Between July 1 and August 31 every French wage earner takes a three or four week break. It is referred to, not without irony, as 'la transhumance'. —Ed.]

of the system. They are like sea-side council estates or natural concentration camps. As H. M. Enzensberger says, on such sites you find 'police-style regimentation of the compulsorily sited tents and the rule of order, enforced by the camp director'.[15] Thus, little by little, order and administration creep back into periods of physical 'liberty' in 'free' nature. The order enforced in holiday camping sites recalls or anticipates another kind of camp, also sited in the depths of nature . . . and surrounded with real barbed wire.

Physical leisure activities in the 'leisure civilisation' are thus a symbol of an immense craving to get away – to escape from a totalitarian world. Such activities are a popular version of the small towner's dream of South-Sea islands, or the suburbanite's longing for exotic places. To go to the sea-side or to go skiing amounts to recognition of the fact that the city is uninhabitable – literally hellish. Physical leisure activities serve to paper over this reality which the ideologists of leisure seem to regard as the inevitable fate of humanity. Industrial, urban labour, which appears to be inevitable in any modern civilisation, has to be compensated for by activities which enable people to regain their vitality. That is the theory behind the *Draft Sports Doctrine*:

> 'When a man is subject to cumbersome structures' [such as the state or the CRS for example! —J.-M. B.], lives at an infernal pace and is constantly tried by noise, his only thought is to escape from the frequently inhuman cities where he is cooped up. The dream of open air and of getting back to nature is dramatically reflected in the development of camping, the growing number of people buying houses in the country and the rush to get away at weekends and holiday times.'[16]

But anyone who is exhausted by his work and imagines he can escape this carceral universe by hiding away in the country in fact comes up against the very same masters he is controlled and managed by at work in the city, namely, big capital and the state. Nature, which he took for a secret hideaway, turns out to be another field for exploitation by capital and the tourist industry.

15. H. M. Enzensberger, *Culture ou mise en condition*, Julliard, Paris, 1965, p. 170.
16. *Essai de doctrine du sport*, op. cit., p. 53.

The leisure pursuits he thought he had chosen freely turn out to be just what was on offer on the tourist market, controlled by state policy. Nature and physical leisure activities are colonised by big capital. The deterioration of beauty spots, land grabbing, the destruction of animal and plant life and the contraction of living space are all products of the setting up of commercialised tourist areas and the repressive socialisation of nature by capital – even nature does not escape this process. People are expected to spend their holidays in an alienated nature, or in other words, to rebuild their strength in an environment which is claimed to be 'natural' but which is in fact carved up and run according to the norms of the city. *The private ownership of nature* is progressively turning the greater part of the countryside and most holiday resorts into dumping grounds – public parks for the masses. The customer of the leisure industry is supposed to regain his lost energy in a pseudo-nature, alienated to capital, artificially exoticised and presented like a series of picture post-cards. The damaged individual seeks relief in destroyed and vandalised natural surroundings. The universal need to escape to nature, the flight from the artificial city environment, from the terroristic work situation, the development of open air sports, such as boating, sailing, riding, skiing and underwater fishing, the rush to the natural parks, the search for quiet spots to spend holidays – *these are all indications that organic relationships with nature have been deeply disturbed.*[17] *In its turn, the relationship with nature becomes a repressive one.* Nature becomes a site for rubbish dumps, a place where the individual works off his animal-killing instinct – an amusement park where the masses find themselves in the same atmosphere as in their city council estates.

Granted, the desire which tourism feeds on, the aspiration to go on holiday and get back to nature, is, as Enzensberger notes, a desire for the joys of freedom. But the apparatus has managed to absorb this desire and turn it against the individual. For the apparatus imposes both the aims and objectives, the content and

17. K. Marx discusses this question in the *Manuscripts of 1844*, in K. Marx/F. Engels *Collected Works*, Vol. 3, Lawrence & Wishart, London, 1975, p. 276. He speaks of nature as man's 'inorganic body'. 'Man', he says, '*lives* on nature – means that nature is his *body*, with which he must remain in continuous interchange if he is not to die.' Further on, he speaks of 'the true rebirth of nature', which prefigures Marcuse's thesis of the 'pacification of nature'.

the form of holidays, leisure pursuits and travel.

'Tourism', says Enzensberger, 'proves that we have got used to considering as freedom what is really a fraud into which the masses are driven. In contenting ourselves with the thought of the return ticket in our pockets, we are accepting that freedom is not the aim at all — in fact, we have already forgotten what freedom is.'[18]

The apparatus is now seeking to systematise this ignorance of freedom on a massive scale by proposing to establish structures for the reception of people during leisure time. The state proposes to set up such structures in order to 'cope with the need for everyday, weekend and holiday leisure activity'. These are the *'Weekend and Holiday Sports Centres'*. 'Such centres could be used at the weekend by city dwellers to give them the chance to escape and relax in natural surroundings.'[19] What is planned are huge parks for sports and open air activities established on selected natural sites, surrounded by specially equipped 'protected zones', camp sites etc. Needless to say, these centres would be controlled by state officials. As the *Draft Sports Doctrine* states:

'The presence of a *specialised management* is indispensable if these centres are to have the dynamic life and influence which can alone ensure their success . . . The profession of leisure activity leader should be recognised as a social necessity . . . the state should therefore set up the necessary establishments for the training of competent holiday leaders.'[20]

As if curbing freedom of movement in nature and parking people in managed leisure camps were not enough, the state also seeks to control and programme the *content* of people's leisure activity through 'monitors', qualified in 'leadership', with the jobs of controlling holidaymakers. As we can see, the idea behind the existing practice of putting special police officers on the beaches and at swimming pools is making headway, and seems to be becoming institutionalised in civilian life. Soon sporting activity will be made legally compulsory — the worker will be *obliged* to get fresh air in order to recuperate and recover his vitality.

18. H. M. Enzensberger, op. cit., p. 174.
19. *Essai de doctrine du sport*, p. 63 (our emphasis).
20. Ibid., p. 64 (our emphasis).

Already the *Draft Sports Doctrine* clearly states that leisure time should not be disposed of freely as people see fit. Leisure should be beneficial, profitable, active and productive.

> 'Rest time merits (sic)holidays which should not be identified with *lazy inactivity*, likely to be a bad influence on young people and in any case, neither desirable nor beneficial for anyone. Active leisure pursuits, practised in moderation, are necessary for true physical and mental relaxation.'[21]

The mask is thrown off! Young people no longer have the right to experience the joys of the 'right to laziness',[22] but instead must occupy their minds and bodies with 'healthy' leisure activities.

At this point, the mythology of the leisure civilisation joins up with another, much more pervasive mythology: that of moral order and of order in general. The order in question in leisure activity involves generalised regimentation of the masses for summer exercises on a grand scale, so that a healthy, virile, happy and hardworking population can spend its free time efficiently under the enlightened guidance of qualified monitors and managers. Mass scouting is round the corner, taking us towards physical and moral 'Health' – 'A healthy mind in a healthy body': the watchword of a new style Vichy régime.

Jean-Marie Brohm, August 1968.

21. Ibid., p. 59 (our emphasis).
22. P. Lafargue, *The Right to be Lazy*, Charles H. Kerr, Chicago, 1907. The French edition, Maspéro, Paris 1965 has an introduction by J-M. Brohm.

The Olympic Opiate*

– 'The Olympic stadium – the centre of the world for a fortnight.' (*l'Equipe*, 26.8.72)

– 'The Games should be the universal festival of sport: both a measure of, and a contributor to human progress. They should continue to be fertile ground for international exchanges where the young people of the world can meet each other: a living example of the possibility of peaceful coexistence between countries with different social systems. The Games can make a contribution towards peace, the fight against racial discrimination and better understanding among men. That is why the Communists defend the Olympics against those who are seeking to scuttle them.' (René Piquet, member of the Political Bureau of the PCF, *L'Humanité*, 5.8.72)

– 'This festival of peace, this great gathering of world youth: the Olympic games.' (*l'Aurore*, 26.8.72)

The shots fired by the Palestinian commandos put an end to the myth of the Olympic truce. But before this, many events had seriously upset the idea that the Games were non-political and non-aligned – about 60 people were wounded during an anti-war demonstration on Saturday, September 2nd. 'The great festival of sport foundered in tragedy,' said *Europe No. 1* . . . But, 'the Olympic peace is stronger than the terrorists' crimes', declared the International Olympic Committee spokesperson. So what is

*A slightly modified version of a dossier which appeared in *Politique Hebdo* (7.9.1972).

this 'Olympic peace', this con-trick, this smokescreen, this myth powerful enough to give rise to a unanimous chorus of protest from the entire world?

It seems to us more necessary than ever before, if only from the point of view of political morality, to show just how fallacious the ideology behind the Olympic Games is, how it serves to maintain the balance of forces between the great powers and how it con-tributes to the gigantic operation of regimentation and de-humanisation which is behind the entire practice of a certain type of sport. To put the facts on record without distortion is not to come out in favour of a bloodbath. We are merely seeking to show that political reality is everywhere and that the belief in 'the great disinterested festival', shared by both the right and left wings of French and indeed any other nation's politics, is an illusion.

Politics pervades the Olympics from top to bottom. Previously we suspected this to be the case – now we can be certain.

There exists a vast national concensus, encompassing both the progressive and reactionary press, government and opposition, concerning this 'time of peace and human fraternity', this 'island of culture', this 'disinterested festival of youth' which is now re-garded as tarnished. The entire country watched open-mouthed the exploits of 'our oarsmen, boxers, gymnasts and marksmen, our modern pentathlon trio and our hockey team . . .', as *L'Humanité* put it (27.8 72).

Faced with this holy alliance of national and international class-collaboration, militants must be armed to de-mystify the domi-nant ideology in sport, exposing it as a camouflage of social reality, as false political consciousness. This, at a time when the dykes are being bombed in Vietnam and show-trials are still being staged in Eastern Europe. We must expose the historical amalgam, made by Olympic ideology in the name of 'eternal sport', between the Games of antiquity and the modern Olympics. This is invoked to support the claim that sport is over and above history and the class-struggle – part of the heritage of humanity. We must criticise the conceptual confusion and sloppiness of those who use the word 'sport' to refer to any kind of physical activity, from a leisurely bicycle ride to a race against the clock in the Tour de France, from kicking a ball about among friends to a championship football match, or from a commuter's little sprint to catch his bus to the 100 metres final in the Olympics.

A Bit of History

What is referred to as 'modern sport' appeared with the advent of large-scale industry during the period of the rise of English capitalism in the 18th and 19th centuries. The development of sport went hand in hand with that of world capitalism. The first Olympics in Athens in 1896 (the return to the origins of the Games), those in Paris in 1900, in Saint Louis in 1904 and in London in 1908, were all in fact sporting appendages to Universal Exhibitions where the economic world powers were gathered. But it was soon realised that the Games themselves could be a source of profits and be integrated into the framework of a strategy for economic expansion. Today, for the Munich Games, a monopolistic state bloc has been formed, comprising the German Olympic Committee, the Games organisation Committee which includes banks, insurance companies, local and national industrial firms, the Bavarian state, parties, churches and so on, the German Sport Aid Association constituted by Coca-Cola, BMW, Dresdner Bank, Stern magazine etc. This bloc provides an institutional framework for investment for the benefit of the German economy and German prestige. A great disinterested festival? Some people will say anything!

The influence of profit in so-called amateur sport, and the converse process whereby sport is employed for commercial advertising, lead to the transformation of champions into the official representatives of the firms providing their equipment, and to the transformation of the Olympics, together with all other major sports meetings, into a confrontation, via their representatives, between industrial firms, fighting for domination of the market.

Peaceful coexistence

The principle justification advanced for the Games is the hypocritical concept of peaceful coexistence, which is really no more than an attempt to maintain the status quo between the great powers. Alexey Kosygin wrote to the IOC and to the participants in the Munich Games in the following terms:

'The Olympic Games in our time have become a great stimulant for physical, cultural and sporting development and an important way of bringing together sportsmen from the six continents of the globe. The Soviet state follows the Leninist principles of peace and peaceful coexistence in its foreign policy, and supports all forces and movements which struggle for mutual understanding between peoples and for peace.' (l'Humanité, 26.8.72.)

Sport has thus become the perfect image, the model of true national and international peaceful cooperation. American imperialism is no longer an enemy to be brought down but a partner to be met and defeated on the politically harmless 'ground' of the sports stadium.

Are the 'little balls which bring friendship', of the Chinese table-tennis players the forerunners of ping-pong or volley-ball diplomacy? Will the present close contacts between the Chinese sports authorities, the international sports federations and the IOC be sealed by the readmittance of China into the IOC and her participation in the Games in Montreal in 1976 and . . . in Moscow in 1980? G. Onesti, president of the Italian Olympic Committee, reported, on his return from China, that 'sport as a way of life and a form of education is employed in an exemplary way in China. It is obvious that in the Peoples' Republic of China not only is Olympic sport as we in the IOC understand it, alive and well, but the desire of the Chinese to come back into the great Olympic family is very clear.' (l'Equipe, 2.8.72.) Is Signor Onesti just indulging in wishful thinking? We can only hope so.

Sport and work

When they engage in 'sporting leisure activities', workers are practising a physical activity closely related to the world of work, based on a form of thought which prepares for and justifies the type of relationship with the body which is imposed by industrial labour.

The aim of this type of competition is to strive for the record, representing maximum output. This necessitates the intensive labour of training which, at the level of preparation for the Olympics, can only be compared with the most soul-destroying work pace on an assembly line. The champion becomes a producer of performances and records and his labour no longer belongs to him. He is totally governed by his trainer, a veritable foreman, whose sole aim is to increase the productivity of his athletes.

Just before the Games a girl appeared on TV in tears. 'Despite my performances they haven't selected me – it's not right. If only you knew the conditions of training – I fought as hard as possible – there's no reason – I can't understand it.' An emotional moment on the mid-day programme. The interviewer, ill at ease, could not quite understand why this note of doubt had crept in amidst the general euphoria. Here's why: *this was a woman whose body no longer belonged to her*: a machine, a guinea-pig, anything but a woman. Isn't that rather disturbing?

Present day sports practice, *even at the lower levels of competition*, requires a truly frenetic muscular effort. Not only does training proper go to crazy lengths but even the biological equilibrium of the athlete is organised through a vast process of conditioning. The sportsman is completely alienated to an apparatus of medical operators who work on him as they would a guinea-pig in a laboratory. For several years now, the sex of sportswomen suspected of being rather too virile has been checked with hormonal or cell tests. Drug tests are being carried out with increasingly police-style methods, particularly in cycling. The athlete has to submit the most intimate of his metabolic functions to the urine managers.

To help the athlete stand up to competition he is prepared like a race-horse for a big race. Depending on the event, technicians administer a whole range of chemical treatments, going from amphetamines to anabolic steroids, the former to do away with fatigue and the latter to artificially build up muscle tissue. Although, in theory, these procedures are forbidden, they are everyday practice. They are a good indication of the direction sport is going in at present. The system is creating *monsters* (the weight-lifters), running, jumping and swimming *machines*, and *experimental creations* (especially in E. Germany) who have totally internalised the principle of maximum productivity.

The entire technocratic ideology, whether in its imperialist or stalinist form, of the good machine – cybernetic, productive and functionally integrated – is expressed in pure form in sport: the experimental science of human output. This is what lies behind the highly reified language of sport which constantly identifies man with the machine. For example, in *France Soir* (27.8.72), a swimmer is described as, 'built like a speed boat: broad torso, slim legs, thin buttocks, big hands and huge feet. His main asset – a fantastic leg kick which makes him look as if he is driven by an outboard motor.'

The result is that like the worker, the athlete is completely alienated to a process over which he has no control and by which he is dominated. Very often he is directly subordinated to his trainer or manager. He is in their hands. And when that is not enough he goes to consult the sages and healers. Not only do the trainers do all the thinking for him, but even his body no longer belongs to him: it belongs to science. In the Stalinised Eastern European countries this science has been called 'humanics': the 'science of physical output at all ages of life'. The sportsman has become so fragile and complex that he must be kept under continuous medical surveillance. As *Le Monde* (24.8.72) put it: 'The sportsman has paradoxically become a fragile creature, constantly threatened with muscle failure and often so worried by his fitness that he confesses all his anxieties to his doctor.' You only have to look at the number of 'injured' in the French team . . . the whole country hangs on every fitness bulletin of a Pani or a Tracanelli . . . our boys have got problems.

In the race after maximum productivity anything goes. The champion's life-style is drastically rationalised: no drink, no sexual relations, special diets. These are all, of course, 'sacrifices accepted in the interests of . . .'. *The body itself is 'Taylorised'.* All unnecessary gestures are avoided – there is only a limited number of ways of jumping as high as possible. It is worth noting in passing that Taylor himself took sport as his starting point for his studies on the rationalisation of productive human labour.

For the athletes, the Olympics are also a way of moving up the social ladder. The athlete submits to this model of social advancement: individual promotion through success in a sport.

The Olympic ideal

The notion of a *truce* is fundamental to the ideology of sport. To quote M. Maheu, director of UNESCO:

> 'The idea of a truce is an important element of the Olympic ideal. Quarrels, misunderstandings, conflicts and hatreds should be suspended during the Games. The combination of an eagerness to win and a respect for the rules which we find in sports competition leads naturally to greater mutual respect, understanding and even friendship. Yes, sport is a truce. In our technological societies ruled by the iron law of labour, in which a man is only

what he possesses, and possesses only what he has earned, blessed is the game which fills our leisure time with free riches. Amid the antagonisms and conflicts of our time which is dominated by the will to power and by pride, blessed is the respite which brings respect and friendship.' (*UNESCO, Courrier*, January 1964.)

There it is in black and white. Beneath the armchair philosophising and the pseudo-literary turns of phrase, this quotation expresses an idea whose hypocrisy is not the sole property of UNESCO.

A look at the press speaks volumes about these Games, the aim of which is to 'crystallise peace between men and nations', in the words of Jacques Goddet in *l'Equipe* (26.8.72). The aim is to give credence to the idea of a break in the international class struggle, of an example of mutual understanding between men of good will motivated by the spirit of sportsmanship. 'The Games contribute to the cause of the democratisation of sport and thus, at the end of the day, they aid the cause of democracy and socialism.' (*Cahiers du Communisme*, January 1969.) Like the peaceful co-existence on which it is modelled, the Olympic truce is designed to lull the exploited masses and peoples into passivity. Its real significance is political: class collaboration at every level.

National unity

Look at what the Independent Republican deputy, B. Destremeau has to say in *Le Monde* (28.8.70):

'All peoples need a safety valve, and nationalism in sport seems to have the fewest drawbacks. Nor should we forget the admirable efforts made by so many athletes whose dream is to be selected for their country. The ambition to wear the national colours is a crucial incentive which contributes to character building.'

Enough to send shivers down your spine! Here we have the best way to unite the French people behind their flag and their team. Not only do the champions serve as propagandists for national prestige abroad, but the bourgeois state also uses sport and its heroes to bring the masses to an identification with the state and its policies. Both the mass media and the Communist Party, through *l'Humanité* and the FSGT, play a key role in the development of national identity and chauvinism.

What could be better than a good Cup Final, a good Tour de France or Rugby Tournament to put social conflicts on one side and bring together 'all Frenchmen' in front of the TV screen – exploiters and exploited all worshipping together in the one true sporting faith. 'The spectacle of sport is the modern form of folk drama, enabling repressed passions and instincts to be let off without danger or guilt, purged through sport.'[1]

The Superman

Closely linked to this proto-fascist manipulation of peoples, one of the dominant myths of sport and the Olympics is that of the *superman-champion*. These men, like so many mythical heroes, achieve perfection by realising the fulness of their potential, a perfection surpassed with each new Olympics, as the limits of human capacity are pushed back. The permanent function of this cult of the élite is to bring the masses to identify with this sort of superman. Under Mussolini or Stalin, stadiums were full of such disturbingly powerful, statuesque figures. Nowadays we have the star system. Figures like Pele, Killy, Mark Spitz or Borzov fulfil the function of physical, emotional and social reference points for youngsters. 'The champion is a force of attraction for young people. He wins their admiration. His successes and triumphs set their imaginations loose. Experience proves conclusively that performances by the élite always give rise to a renewal of interest in sporting activity among young people.'[2]

Elitist sport is also deeply imbued with the idea of surpassing one's own limitations, which is an integral part of the positivist myth of 'progress': the myth of the indefinite progression of human performances, possibilities and productive capacity. 'Sport is a factor of advancement because its essence is a striving after performances and records: the will to surpass oneself, taken to the extreme.'[3]

All classes in society are affected. 'The gods of the stadium are going into combat', headlined the *Parisien Libéré* (28.8.72), echoing the title of the film of the 1936 Berlin Olympics, *The Gods of the Stadium*. These were the Games of course which provided the Nazis with a political propaganda platform. 'The champions

1. *Essai de doctrine du sport*, Haute Comité des Sports, Paris, 1965, p. 71.
2. Op. cit., p. 73.
3. Op. cit., p. 15.

are the guides of the human race', declared *l'Ecole et la Nation*, a PCF monthly magazine (June 1969).

'Sport, including competitive sport, is a world in which free men thrive. An athlete who overcomes his own limitations because he realises that this is the way to fulfil himself is the very opposite of an alienated individual. The profound virtues of sport serve as an example of the kind of society we wish to construct.' (*Syndicalisme*, the paper of the CFDT, September 1972.)

Our critique of sport is not nihilist or intellectualist as the Communist Party claims. If today we criticise sport, the dominant capitalist and bureaucratic form of physical education, as repressive and alienating, *it is precisely because competitive sport does not educate the body but mutilates it.* (To see this you only have to look at some of the monsters produced by the Olympic Games.) The charge levelled against competitive sport stems from this very concrete fact.

'Physical education' is held up as the perfect form of development of the body, in that it is meant to permit the all-round development of the individual's physical, intellectual, moral and cultural talents, the full expression of the personality and so on. The Communists and the Soviet ideologues even go as far as to claim that the sportsman is a forerunner of the 'complete man' Marx wrote about. However reality is rather different.

In fact the opposite is true. As a result of systematic training and competition, sportsmen are increasingly becoming specialists. They are confined to a narrow field of sports practice, often to the exclusion of all other sports. It is considered highly inadvisable, for example for a runner to play rugby or football. Far from being a complete individual, the sportsman lives a narrow, compartmentalised existence. His job is to execute one movement according to a stereotyped and mechanical routine, just like an assembly line worker in fact. The sportsman himself is like a machine tool — a sort of human power unit. Witness the ravings of Roland Passevant in *l'Humanité* (26.8.72): 'These men and women we see limbering up, running, jumping and sprinting are clearly the best human machines available.'

The 'cyberntrope'

Far from being a liberating, broadening or creative form of individual development, sport is a colossal process of alienation. The individual is screwed down to the competitive machine of the institution of sport. He is a victim of the 'cretinism of work', described by Marx, like a worker dulled by the hellish work pace and harrassed by his foreman. A long or middle distance runner puts in as much as 30 or 40 kilometres a day in training. A swimmer manages up to 10 to 14 kilometres a day in the pool. A weight lifter lifts tons of iron etc. We can say that sportsmen are being turned into cybernetic robots. To borrow H. Lefebvre's expression, the 'cyberntrope' has arrived.

The state sportsman is totally subordinated to the institution of sport and in particular to the administrative hierarchy of sporting organisations such as the Olympic Committee, sports Federations, the Olympic preparation department and so on. Even the most intimate details of his private life are controlled. Far from being free, he is a conscript in the mobile sports army. The discipline to which he is submitted is of the military type. It is no accident that one Colonel Crespin is the boss for Olympic preparation in France. Recently, in the Olympic village, the athletics manager, Robert Bobin, gave the following sermon to his Olympic flock:

'You shouldn't need me to tell you that you have made too many sacrifices to spoil everything by fooling around here. You will have to go to bed early, without disturbing the others. We will be very strict. The first one to play the fool will be put on the first plane back to Paris. This isn't a holiday you know.' (*Le Monde*, 26.8.72.)

For athletes from Eastern Europe the policing and administrative control goes to grotesque lengths, reminiscent of certain well known passages in George Orwell's *1984*. Soviet athletes for example may only be interviewed when accompanied by their 'trainers', who are in turn supervised by an 'interview officer'.

Needless to say, whatever country they represent, no athletes dare express a political opinion other than the official line. The French prime minister Messmer made sure the French team received his 'briefing' before the Munich Games: 'Very best wishes for success. I hope the team gets good results all round, for all of you in every discipline have worked hard. I trust that each and every one of you will show his mettle.' And Comiti frequently recalled that athletes who travelled abroad were representatives of France . . . the implications under the Pompidou régime need no further explaining!

In this bureaucratic world there is a special staff to take care of 'moral order'. The Olympic village is like an adolescents' holiday camp or a convent in which sexual repression is made an institution. The village is segregated, the women's quarters being separated from the mens' by the famous 'anti-flirting fence'. The few gaps in the fence are barred by 'strapping lads in light-blue uniforms, like so many Cerberuses guarding the gates of hell' (l'Equipe). L'Aurore (14.8.72) published a picture of a woman dressed like a Salvation Army Major, whose job it was to ensure that 'the young misses got up to no mischief', by patrolling the women's quarters. Whichever way you turn, you meet the same bureaucratic idiocy and childishness. The athletes must 'go to bed early', behave 'responsibly', not 'get tired' and so it goes on. Of course, as the ineffable Robert Bobin reminded us (Le Monde 26.8.72): 'The athletes must be protected from the dangers that can be encountered in such a gathering of ten thousand young people.'

So beneath the nonsense about sport developing free, adult citizens, we find athletes who are imprisoned, indoctrinated, regimented and repressed. So much for the idea of self-fulfilment, development of the personality and the exemplary individual held up by the bourgeoisie and unreservedly backed by the Communist Party with its customary jingoistic verve.

An ideological apparatus

Sport is part of the mechanism of the bourgeois state – a transmission belt for capitalism. Sport has become monopoly state sport. This fact bears repetition for the benefit of the PCF and other advanced democrats who seek to democratise sport and build a democratic sports movement within a democratic state. The Communist Party's Olympic cretinism is complemented by the sporting utopianism of the 'labourites' of the Labour Sports and Gymnastics Federation (FSGT), the sports section of the CGT.

Sport is an ideological apparatus. Its structures – federations, clubs, the Olympic Committee etc. – are closely tied to the state apparatus which often appoints or 'nominates' their officers. The state itself promotes an official approach to sport, the *Draft Sports Doctrine*, which is put in to practice through a special structure: the Ministry for Youth and Sport. Top-level athletes are state servants with the job of promoting the régime's official propaganda. (See for example, Jazy and Goitschel, representatives of the Gaullist party; Mimoun, a veteran of the Gaullist movement *et al*).

For some time now there has been a tendency in France for the institutions of sport and the armed forces to be fused into a national sports/military bloc, in which soldiers are all good sportsmen and sportsmen are considered as the soldiers of the track, decorated as national heroes, received at the Presidential Palace and the rest. The 'new society' dreamed up by sporting Gaullists like Chaban-Delmas boils down to a national state monolith in which all the institutions of bourgeois society are cemented together through the practice of sport, held to be a source of national harmony. This is the idea behind the so-called educative role of the army. The Gaullist sports doctrine argues: 'Sport enables the army to play a role of continuity in relation to the family, the schools or enterprises. Sports brings the army into cooperation with clubs, local authorities and companies, through the provision of equipment and instructors. In short, in social terms, sport proves to be a strong link between the army and the nation.'[4] Work, Fatherland, Family . . . Army, Sport!

This organic link between sport and the state reflects the fact that in order to maintain its domination, the bourgoisie has always used sport as a means of controlling the working class ideologically, whether it be Company sport, sport in the army or sport 'for the whole nation'. To this end the bourgeoisie has established state or para-state structures to regiment young people. For the bourgeoisie, sport is an ideal instrument of mass control.

The aim is to divert young people on a mass scale towards the practice of sport within the framework provided by clubs, sports federations and various para-state bodies. For the bourgeoisie sport has the explicit role of de-politicising, intellectually dulling and militarising youth. Especially as regards spare time sport, the ruling class seeks to impose an inoffensive, neutral and conformist prac-

4. Op. cit., p. 43.

tice. Their watchword is 'sport not politics'. Following the events of May/June 1968, the bourgeoisie unanimously agreed that if only the students would do a bit more sport and work off their aggression on the playing fields, they would be less inclined to challenge the system . . . Throw the discus rather than bricks!

Brain washing

Bourgeois ideology is only effective in so far as it is internalised by the masses, establishing itself as a standard form of behaviour, rooted in automatic, everyday reflexes and experienced as false consciousness. At present the masses are steeped in bourgeois sports ideology. Using an expression coined by W. Reich in *the Mass Psychology of Fascism*, the main way in which sport is 'anchored in the masses' is through a process of imprinting certain behaviour patterns on them. Sport has become part of the 'mass psyche', embodied in ritual and obsessive practices and constituting a sort of mental boundary, a blind spot or an internalised moral code.

The scope of the sports phenomenon is due above all to the saturation of the mass media (newspapers, advertising, etc.), with the sports spectacle. Sporting events attract huge crowds. The Tour de France, major football matches, boxing contests or the Olympics themselves attract hundreds of thousands of spectators and millions of TV viewers. The gigantic scale of sports events aids the process of reducing the population to a servile mass. Throughout the year, the hearts and minds of the masses are assaulted with sports contests of every shape and form which are then reported in inimitable ideological style in the major newspapers and on TV. In this way sport provides a smokescreen, diverting people from their real problems.

In countries dominated by imperialism in alliance with local oligarchies, victims of underdevelopment and pauperisation (Brazil, Greece, Portugal, Spain etc.), sport is an effective means of manipulating the masses who are brutally repressed by military or fascist dictatorships. In Latin American countries for instance, football is a veritable system of government for the local ruling cliques.* Football, often accompanied by large scale betting, be-

---

*See, for example, the last article in the present volume, *The Appeal for a Boycott of the Organisation, by Argentina, of the Football World Cup.*

comes a real opiate of the people, enabling them to forget the trials of everyday life and close their eyes to the police terror – their idols are sportsmen such as Pele. Another type of ideological imprinting takes the form of stereotypes of 'social participation'. The purest expression of class collaborationist ideology is the notion of 'partnership between capital and labour', of 'dialogue between the two sides of industry' which is behind the social contract policy. The bourgeoisie aims to convince people that really there are no such things as antagonistic social classes. Instead there are 'social partners' who can come to agree on tacit or explicit contracts by 'playing the game' on 'neutral terrain' under an 'impartial referee', namely the state, while 'abiding by agreed rules' which embody the bourgeoisie's idea of the proper norms of 'fair play'. In one form or another this type of reasoning can be heard in every haunt of employers or government politicians. What is worse is that respectable, reformist and integrated trade unionism accepts this type of social contract policy.

This model is faithfully reproduced in miniature within the practice of sport: loyal partners, agreed rules, impartial referee, neutral terrain and so on. Sports ideology makes a key contribution to the practical, concrete implantation of participatory ideas – a fact which is not lost on its promoters. The *Draft Sports Doctrine* for example, blandly declares: '*Sport produces respect for the loyally established hierarchy,* and encourages a sense of equality, solidarity and interdependence. It is undoubtedly an excellent apprenticeship in human relations and a remarkable school of sociability.'[5] The 'Official Instructions' issued to physical education teachers go even further: '. . . sport is practised according to rules, and encourages behaviour based on the generally accepted values of society'. This surely speaks for itself.

Jean-Marie BROHM
Jean-Michel DAMIEN
Claude MAURIN
August 1972.

5. Op. cit., p. 24 (our emphasis).

The Olympic Games and the Imperialist Accumulation of Capital*

These days, major sports contests give rise to bitter competition, both beforehand and alongside the events themselves, between cities and countries anxious to secure for themselves the financial market and commercial business that such events entail.

1. Competition Between the Great Powers and Small Countries

Industrial firms and financial and commercial groups have not been slow to grasp the advantages of organising the Olympics or other international meetings. That is why capitalist enterprises push countries and local authorities into putting themselves forward for this role. They vaunt the economic gains for regional development and hold out the promise of financial aid in the hope of 'encouraging' favourable decisions. The same capitalist institutions infiltrate the mechanisms of sports organisation itself, by facilitating the financial side of things. *Nowadays, finance capital has made its way into the sports apparatus through advertising, organisational assistance and very often as a financial backer.*

A structural osmosis is thus developing between sports institutions and banks, tourist offices, travel agents, airlines, regional development bodies, property companies, big industrial firms and so on. This sports/economic complex is characteristic of present day developments within state monopoly capitalism. The complex functions as a whole, in which the interests of the different ele-

*This essay developed out of an article which appeared in *Le Chrono Enrayé*, No. 8, op. cit.

ments are combined and mutually reinforce each other.

The all-out competition between the bourgeoisie of different countries is fully reflected at the level of sport. The great powers tend increasingly to monopolise the sphere of sport for their own benefit, to the detriment of small countries. This attempt to monopolise sporting activity is motivated by the profits and prestige to be gained from sport. Major sports competitions, and in particular the Olympics, are one element of the international competition in which the nations are engaged.

Such competition takes two forms: Firstly, within the camp of the great powers themselves, which compete amongst themselves. Secondly, it operates between the major imperialist powers and the small subordinate countries which can no longer stand up to the competition.

Major international sports meetings such as the Olympics require a considerable mobilisation of capital. Huge financial investments are required to help to boost economic activity, to encourage trade, to bring commercial business and urban and industrial development to the regions concerned. Small countries, especially in the third world, cannot last the pace of this economic and sports rivalry, or if they do, only by releasing considerable sums in the form of national investments which call on the entire economic energies of the country.

Thus the world economic hierarchy has direct consequences on a nation's level of competitivity in sport. Today only the top nations can take on the organisation of major international competitions like the Olympics. This hierarchy naturally reasserts itself when it comes to choosing the country and city to organise the Olympic Games.

As M. Castaing remarks (*Le Monde*, 15.5.70) concerning the choice of city for the 1976 Games:

'it remains the case that the organisation of the Games has been assigned to the cities of powerful nations. It is hardly likely, now that the Olympics have become an affair of State, that Canada or the US will need encouraging to out-do the grand scale of the Sapporo Games in Japan or the Munich Games in Germany. And these countries in turn hope to go one better than France and Mexico, who in turn. . . . Similarly, it is unrealistic to expect that the first Communist candidate, Moscow, could possibly be content to return to greater simplicity in 1980.'

Montreal in Quebec was chosen as the Olympic city for the summer Games in 1976 because the city possessed both high quality sports facilities and a solid urban infrastructure, largely built for the Universal Exhibition in 1967, which attracted considerable amounts of capital and required major investments. 'These could not have been undertaken by a city in a small country.' (M. Castaing, *Le Monde*, 14.5.70.)

Consequently the economic relationship of forces determines choices in sport, in so far as small countries are either unable or find it increasingly difficult to keep up with the escalation of the Olympics. The case of Amsterdam is an interesting example. The capital city of Holland, where the Games were held in 1928, would today be quite unable to stage a socio-economic event on the scale of a modern Games without running into excessive expenditure. This fact was admitted by the Dutch Minister for Culture, Leisure and Social Action, Dr. Klompe, in his opening speech to the 69th session of the International Olympic Committee. 'The organisation of the Olympics requires financial sacrifices which are beyond the means of a small country like mine. I am also bearing in mind the right of the third world to stage the Games.' (*Le Monde*, 15.5.70.)

2. The expansion strategy of capital and sports competition

Countries and cities seeking to land the deal increasingly intervene as financial and economic pressure groups within sports organisations. Sports events are the objects of battles between powerful economic interests. J. Meynaud realistically draws attention to this fact:

'This is particularly the case for the Olympics, not forgetting the weight of commercial considerations which lie behind the bitter struggle between cities to obtain the staging of an Olympics . . . But behind these cities are their states, since in most cases the cities are unable to meet the basic expenditure involved in such events without substantial state subsidy. The role of travelling salesman played by the leading citizens of these cities, not always in a particularly dignified way, is a good indication of the scope of the material interests which hang on the eventual choice.'[1]

Such organic cooperation between the various interested parties
within the capitalist state-sports complex was shown up for example, during the Mexico Games. As J. Meynaud reports: 'Commercial interests were quick to seize on the advantages to be gained
from this sort of sports fever. Banks opened special "sports current
accounts" where people were invited to deposit the money they
would need to be able to play a respectable part in the Games. The
advertising for many food products played on the theme of "giving
the country the champions it deserves in 1968." '[2] Official organisations launched national fund drives to finance the Games and to
support the 'national sports effort'.

The Winter Olympics at Sapporo in 1972 was an equally good
example of the combination of commercial, diplomatic and banking interests which together form a politico-economic-sports complex. The Sapporo Games gave rise to fierce competition alongside
the events. Japan represented a huge market to be conquered.
Austrian, French, Swiss, German, Canadian and American firms
fought over this market with all the means at their disposal, including the dispute over amateurism. For all the firms connected
with winter sports, the stakes were high. As was noted in a special
supplement in *Le Monde* entitled 'A market to be conquered'
(30.1.72), 'For all concerned the effort is worth it. What is at stake
is the conquest of the biggest winter sports market in the world,
namely Japan. The sale of no less than 16 million pairs of skis
is up for grabs, with all that goes with it.' But over and above
the Japanese market itself there are the US, Canada and soon the
caucasian countries in Central Europe. *The snow has thus become
a source of handsome profits.* French ski exports for example went
from 16 million francs worth in 1966 to 100 million francs worth
in 1971. This spectacular growth was based primarily on the American market. France delivered £5 million worth of skis to the
US in 1970. Nevertheless the competition is stiff, if you consider that Japan exported more than 800,000 pairs of skis in 1971,
mainly to the US, Canada exported 230,000 pairs, W. Germany
170,000 pairs and France a mere 40,000.

1. J. Meynaud, *Sport et politique*, Payot, Paris, 1966, p. 136 (our emphasis).
2. Op. cit. p. 137.

Against this background, the extraordinary efforts of the organising country, Japan, can be understood. Japan was willing to sink the amazing sum of 212 billion yen (over £400 million) in the operation. As has become usual for each Olympics, Japan took the opportunity to improve her material infrastructure: 90 billion yen were spent on the road system, 44 billion on the underground train network and 25 billion on housing, hotels and shops intended for the use of the local population after the Games. In addition, 10 billion yen were spent on the sports facilities themselves and 43 billion were devoted to the development of airports, the building of a Post Office centre and a radio and television centre. Expenditure on this scale fully justifies M. Castaing's description of the Games as a 'publicity circus' (*Le Monde*, 4.2.72).

Evidently, from a political point of view, such sums would have been better used to fight world hunger, illiteracy and underdevelopment, which would have contributed much more effectively to the struggle for 'well-being and peace between peoples', as the official formula has it. For if a balance sheet is drawn up of the last four or five Olympics, the sorry conclusion must be that they form part of an economic system of waste, uncontrolled affluence and the large scale display of luxury, while the rest of the planet is sunk in famine and ignorance. *The Olympics objectively form part of imperialism's development at the expense of the third world. The Games allow third world countries to witness, through the medium of television, the exhibitionist displays of the bourgeois world, gorged and wallowing in the prodigalities of the consumer spectacle.* In other words, Persepholis every four years: circuses and Games for the peoples of the world, oppressed, exploited and enslaved by capital via its states and its cultural and tourist agencies. Just as the sessions of the UN present the spectacle of world diplomacy, so the Olympics stage the leisure activities of the capitalist world: a spectacle of built-in waste, and planned obsolescence; a physical and mental extravaganza put on by one world getting rich at the expense of another. Whether we like it or not, the Olympics endorse and strengthen the imperialist pillage of resources or, to use Marx's expression, the concentration of wealth on the one hand and poverty on the other. In other words, the Games set the seal on the violence of capitalist accumulation throughout the world. The Games themselves are the highest democratic expression of the most refined and subtle form of imperialist accumulation, which, as Rosa Luxemburg put it, 'has the whole world for a stage'. 'Here,' she stresses, 'the methods used are colonial policy, the international loan system, the policy of spheres of influence and war. Unfettered violence, fraud, oppression and pillage are openly deployed.'[3] Olympic accumulation is also an element of the economic and cultural colonisation of the oppressed masses of the third world by international capital, this vampire thirsty for surplus value, as Marx described it. This economic and political violence is refracted through the Olympics, which have become an integral factor in the imperialist process. We can thus accept Rosa Luxemburg's further conclusion that

'in reality, political violence is itself the instrument and the vehicle of the economic process: the dual aspects of accumulation are, at root, one organic phenomenon produced by the conditions of capitalist reproduction. The historical development of capital can only be grasped in the light of these two aspects. Capitalism drips blood from every pore, not just at the time of its birth, but throughout its advance across the world. In this way, through ever more violent convulsions, capitalism brings about its own downfall.'[4]

Although this prognosis does not directly refer to sport, it can perhaps be applied equally well to the Olympic movement. Or in other words, the historical development of the Olympic movement is entirely dependent on the turbulent history of capitalism's career.

Thus, contrary to the well intentioned declarations of the Olympic ideologues, it is no exaggeration to claim that, these days, world and Olympic sport have become entirely subject to international finance capital. What is more, this permanently concealed reality is not just a recent development, although it is more apparent now than in the past. The tendency for international sport to be directly subordinated to big capital has in fact increased steadily since

3. Rosa Luxumburg, *The Accumulation of Capital*, Routledge & K. Paul, London.
4. Op. cit.
   On the question of imperialism, reference can be made to the following works: V. I. Lenin, *Imperialism, the Highest Stage of Capitalism* in *Selected Works* Vol. I Progress, Moscow; N. Bukharin, *Imperialism & World Economy*, Merlin Press, 1972; E. Mandel, *Marxist Economic Theory*, Merlin Press 72; *Critiques de l'Economie Politique*: 'Sur l'Imperialisme', No. 4/5, 1971, Maspéro, Paris.

the turn of the century when the first major sports competitions and in particular the first Olympics were staged. This tendency is an exact reflection of the internationalisation of capital itself, through the export of commodities and of capital, the development of multinational firms and international cartels and trusts. Ardent supporters of sport should be reminded that the early Olympics were in no way pure and disinterested. They were in fact merely sporting side-shows for Universal Exhibitions which involved the big industrial, commercial and financial groups of the period. The Paris Games in 1900 were linked to the Universal Exhibition, the Saint Louis Games in 1904 to the Great Exhibition and Fair, and the London Games in 1908 to the Anglo-French Exhibition.[5] So from the start, the organisation, events and expansionism of modern international sport were closely linked to the affirmation, the extension and the triumph of international capitalism. The Olympic movement in particular was originally nothing more than an epiphenomenon of the celebration of capital and capitalist competition. This gives us an idea of the reality behind the 'return to spiritual values' through sport, and of the material roots of the famous Olympic ideals preached by Coubertin and his successors. As Meynaud notes,

'In fact, despite the pompous declarations of attachment to the spiritual ideals of the Olympics, the Games have almost never been considered, by the cities proposed or chosen to organise them, solely from the point of view of objectives specific to sport. . . . The first Games, held in Athens in 1896, were used by the Greeks to serve the cause of Hellenism and tourist propaganda. The lesson was not lost on future organisers. With only a few exceptions such as the Stockholm Games in 1912, the organising countries have always exploited the event in the interests of national prestige, the promotion of tourism, urban renewal or purely commercial development.'[6]

5. On this question, see R. Vanker, 'l'Histoire des olympiades', *les Cahiers de l'Histoire* No. 78, SEDIP, Paris, September 1968. On the Saint Louis Games, Vanker recalls that 'the Games were merged into the programme of the Exhibition which obviously included big stands and areas reserved for weaving machines, harnesses, early tractors, machine drills and giant threshing machines.' (Op. cit. p. 85.)
6. Op. cit. p. 208.

The Example of Grenoble

The tendency for sport to be integrated into capital's expansion strategy was continued in a particularly clear way at the Winter Olympics held in Grenoble in 1968.

Within the context of the Common Market and the struggle for the European and world sports equipment market, the city of Grenoble, with the backing of the French state, took on the organisation of the Games, with the aim of promoting regional economic development based on tourism and winter sports in the Alps. For Grenoble, the Olympics represented a considerable prize. 'By playing the card of the Grenoble Games, the French government, representing the huge interests tied up in the winter sports industry – including the hotel trade, sports equipment manufacturers, ski instructors, ski lift firms and so on – was aiming at the conquest of the world market, and especially the American market, by this sector of French industry.'[7]

To conquer the world market, the French government was prepared to take on the task of organising the Olympics and commit a considerable amount of money, to the tune of about £135 millions.

The primary objective in this affair was to gain French domination of the market made up of the European winter sports resorts. The main French groups hoped to grab the lion's share of the developing alpine skiing industry. The goal was to profit from the ensuing skiing boom to promote French resorts. At the time, the French Prime Minister, Pompidou, explained the intentions behind the financial effort needed to stage the Games. 'This was a unique opportunity to develop our facilities and give unprecedented publicity to our resorts. This factor, as much as the Games themselves, is what justified the exceptional financial effort.'[8]

This financial effort was not of course without its economic returns. It served to stimulate investment and the development of every kind of facility in the region and in the resorts themselves. The Grenoble Games gave rise to entire chains of hotels, ski resorts, all kinds of sports facility and to the building of a dense network of mountain ski-lifts. As Jean Meynaud stresses,

7. 'Les J. O. d'hiver,' Review: *Education Physique, sport et societé*, Paris, No. 2, p. 3.
8. Op. cit.

the organisation of the Grenoble Games made it possible 'for half a dozen resorts, built over recent decades, to take off thanks to the massive international publicity they received. This explains the decision by Grenoble, which was criticised by the international ski federation's experts, to stage the events on several different sites. This decision is thought to have been backed, if not actually imposed, by the French government out of concern to get the best out of their investments.'[9]

The other aspect of capitalist competition in evidence at Grenoble was the bitter struggle between ski equipment manufacturers for domination of the winter sports market. While the organisers were seeking to attract American and European holidaymakers to French resorts, the ski manufacturers hoped to use the staging of the Olympics as a springboard for the conquest of the ski market. French industrialists skilfully exploited the commercial and advertising possibilities opened up by Killy's success. *The super-champion Killy was an ideal propagandist for French capital in the hunt for foreign markets.* In these circumstances it is easy to see how the Grenoble Games eventually became a matter of national economic importance. Michel Legris (in 'Compétitions sportives et compétitions politiques', *Le Monde*, 8.8.67) went as far as to declare: 'Killy was responsible for the conquest of a new market for French made skis in America'. Similarly, in a study published in *Le Monde* (21.9.71) of the competitive potential of French skis on the alpine market, stress was put on the 'extraordinary influence of Killy, which has produced an extremely favourable public image for French skis'. Certainly!

Another reflection of the sharp competition between manufacturers was the scandal concerning the wearing of brand names by the competitors, which gave rise to so much controversy at the time. In return for buying exclusive rights on this or that well known competitor, the ski manufacturers hoped to profit from the publicity given to the sport. Ski champions were progressively turned into sandwich-board men – the accredited representatives of brands of skis or socks – *turning sports contests into confrontations between industrial firms fighting each other through the intermediary of their sportsmen for domination of the market,* and between trusts or states seeking to impose a monopoly position for the expansion of their capital. Today, major ski competitions

9. Op. cit. pp. 209 and 210 (our emphasis).

such as the winter Olympics, the world championships, the world cup and the like are first and foremost the arena for competition between all the different firms which in one way or another are involved in the rush for 'white gold'. That is why 'ski equipment manufacturers, whose markets are continuously expanding due to the exceptional development of the sport, recruit champions as technical advisers. Publicity gained by the mere presence of such stars amply justifies the cost of their hire'.[10]

From then on, the ski manufacturers can intervene directly or indirectly in the organisation of competitions, through the medium of their champions. They often take on the provision of the material infrastructure. This explains how it is that major ski competitions have become, primarily, huge mobilisations of different capitals seeking to realise surplus value, through the intermediary of their sporting representatives.

Today it is no longer possible to deny either that state monopoly capitalism has penetrated top level sport, including so-called amateur sport or, vice versa, that 'The introduction of sport into the field of commercial promotion . . . creates or consolidates links between producing firms and sports directors and professional athletes,' as J. Meynaud puts it.[11] The most ardent proponents of the ideology of amateurism cannot but admit the reality of capitalist sport, even if they continue to refuse to draw all the practical conclusions that follow. For example, during the Grenoble Games the [then] president of the IOC, Mr. Brundage, noted with somewhat forced naïvety, that:

> 'the winter Olympics have become a massive affair and as such, they have attracted political and commercial attention. Coubertin . . . never thought that governments, rather than using sport for educative purposes, would take it on themselves to train an élite class of athletes in order to promote tourism, sports equipment and sportswear.'[12]

Brundage, who declares his determination to 'eliminate all commercialisation from the Games' and who is desperately trying to defend amateurism, is in fact denying, through a classic process of self-deception or denial of reality in the psychological

10. J. Meynaud, Op. cit. pp. 43 and 44.
11. Op. cit. p. 45.
12. Quoted in the review: *Education physique, sport et societé*.

sense, that major sports competitions such as the Olympics are essentially competitions between states with opposed interests, between rival cities and between firms acting as sports pressure groups. Thereby, Brundage denies that the running of such events is inseparably tied to the clashes of interest which they inevitably produce.

During the 71st session of the IOC, Brundage recognised that 'competitors who allow their names or photographs to be used for the purpose of advertising sports equipment, clothing etc., have become representatives of the manufacturer or retailer'. He therefore declared that he was determined to ban such athletes from taking part, for 'if the participation of such athletes were tolerated, the Games would become merely competitions between firms' representatives rather than between individuals' (*Le Monde*, 16.9.71). But as M. Caistaing noted in the same issue of *Le Monde*, if this rule were applied, 90 per cent of the athletes currently taking part in the Games would have to be disqualified.

So it is in no one's interest to sabotage the Games by banning suspect athletes. On the contrary, everyone concerned has an interest in building the Games up as a world event so that 'sports capital' can expand. Too many interests are involved, starting with the enormous investments needed to organise the Games themselves, for anyone to be 'unreasonable'. Governments are involved in the race after industrial competitivity and the export of commodities and capital. They invest considerable financial, human and organisational resources in Olympic activity. They have every reason to do their utmost to ensure the success of the Olympic operation by promoting a sort of national sports solidarity pact: a version of the war-time national coalition. This involves diplomatic initiatives, advertising campaigns and politico-financial speculation. All these elements are thought up, directed and executed by a general staff, representing all the different organisations involved in the run up to the Olympics.

And Sapporo . . . and Austria

So the long series of compromises arrived at between the capitalist monopolies, sports organisations and the Olympic Committee can be explained by the power of the economic interests at play in top level sport. These different institutions in different ways all depend on top level sport. As we have seen, this has become capitalist state-sport. *Industry, finance capital, the state and sports organisations form a bloc based on shared interests.* So much so that at the end of the day these different partners have no choice but to join together in holy matrimony (of convenience . . .)!

M. Castaing, in an article in *Le Monde* (20.11.71), devoted to the controversy over amateurism, after a subtle explanation of the organisational mechanisms of the Sapporo winter Olympics, at which a compromise had clearly already been reached, wrote: 'The ski industry applies so much pressure, and certain governments are so dependent on the industry, that the various parties concerned are condemned to reach an agreement.'[13]

The organisation of the Sapporo winter Olympics was an outstanding demonstration of the increasingly flagrant contradiction between official Olympic ideology concerning amateurism and the reality of fierce inter-capitalist competition between the winter sports trusts. Despite numerous declarations of intent on amateurism, it is now generally accepted that an amateur member of the French ski team, for example, earns an average of £17,000 a year. This sort of 'shamateurism' which really just amounts to the payment of wages for sporting talent, proves that top level sport of whatever kind has now become a profession. Major competitions are therefore first and foremost confrontations between organisations of professional sportsmen: between sports capitalists seeking to reconcile the reality of profit from sport with the ideology of sport as a disinterested end in itself.

Austria is a good example of the notion of a capitalist state-sports bloc. In Austria, skiing is not just a national sport but also a national industry, involving a variety of interests: tourism, commerce, winter sports products, equipment exports etc. The success of this number one sport is thus essential to the competitivity of this bloc of interests. In order to meet increasingly stiff international competition, particularly from France, Switzerland, W. Germany and even the US, the Austrian state has recently set up the Austrian Ski Pool. This new national association brings together

---

13. M. Castaing reports, (*Le Monde* 20.11.71) that the Ministry for Youth and Sport 'is eager to follow closely the sales of ski equipment abroad.' And recently the sports director publicly regretted the fact that 'France sold 2,000 pairs to Japan, whereas W. Germany supplied 2 million.' As can be seen, there is no incompatibility between sport and the imperatives of the balance of payments! In France as elsewhere . . .

representatives of the Austrian Ski Federation, the Chamber of Commerce and the state, through the ministries for Education, Finance and Trade. This association sponsored by the Austrian state aims to put together a united front of Austrian skiing interests against foreign competition, by developing close cooperation between the officers of the Ski Federation, the ski manufacturers who are already grouped together under the single label 'Austrian Racing Team', and the sports director of the national team. For the last Olympic season, this association was allocated a budget of more than 10 million schillings, 40 per cent of which was provided by the ski manufacturers, 30 per cent by the state and 30 per cent by the Federal Chamber of Commerce (*Le Monde*, 2.9.71).

This organic cooperation between state, ski federation and manufacturers is also to be found in France. The minister for Youth and Sport allocated a subsidy of 1,318,900 francs (£150,000) to the Ski Federation in 1970, and the Federation also received a sum estimated at over a million francs from a pool of manufacturers (*Le Monde*, 9.11.71).

The Olympics business

The 1972 Munich Games showed that 'anything which gets the masses going, sooner or later becomes a matter of money', in the cynical words of the French financial journal *l'Expansion*.[14] The sale of exclusive TV retransmission rights alone brought in a total of £8 millions. During the five years leading up to the Games, Munich was an immense focus of economic and financial activity, subject to a wide range of capitalist pressures. As *l'Expansion* went on to say,

'The games represent a mine of profits. After months of surgery, Munich is just beginning to heal the scars of the underground train construction sites, the 1,400 kilometres of pipeline and the new hospitals, schools and asylums built for the occasion. For several years hundreds of German firms and thousands of workers have been preparing for this 16-day firework display. Not to mention the tons of legs of pork, the tankers full of beer and the millions

14. *l'Expansion*, July/August 1972, p. 54.

of nights worked on shift; nor the property speculation which has pushed land prices up to £50 a square foot. The banks have opened more than 100 new branches since the city was chosen to stage the Olympics, causing Munich to be dubbed "profitopolis". The roof of the stadium alone cost £27 millions. The financing of the Games was a complex affair, the funds coming from various different sources. 100 million silver ten-mark pieces were struck to raise an expected £113 million. The addition of a reference to the Olympics on the German national lottery ticket brought in £62 million. In addition a new lottery, due to operate for 3 years, brought in a further £30 million. The organisation committee even thought up the production of "Waldi" of which about 15 million copies were sold. A special Olympics record was put on sale at 10 marks. The committee also received a series of donations, many of which were far from disinterested. For example, the German car industry supplied up to 2,000 vehicles carrying their own publicity. The provision of the facilities on the site itself was the subject of haggling between the construction corporation (*Olympia Baugesellschaft*) and the private sector.'[15]

The Munich Games were a perfect example of the transformation of the sports apparatus into a state monopoly capitalist bloc, a process which has taken place in every country in the world, especially in the bureaucratic 'socialist' countries. A major sports meeting like the Olympics is an ideal opportunity for industrial and finance capital to valorise huge amounts of capital. In the case of Munich, a complex umbrella organisation was set up, covering several sports and financial organisations. As V. Prokop notes: 'The organisation of the Olympics and of sport in general is the aim and object of a series of sports, industrial and political associations.'[16] For the Munich Games this bureaucratic, para-state complex comprised the German Olympic Committee

---

15. Op. cit.
16. U. Prokop, *Soziologie der olympischen Spiele, Sport und Kapitalismus*, Hanser Verlag, Munich, 1971, p. 113. In general, the modern Olympics, at least since, say, the Melbourne Games of 1956, have been characterised by a combination of three processes. First, there has been a steady increase in the number of nations and athletes taking part. Secondly, the organisation costs have risen dramatically. And thirdly the so-called truce, the 'universal festival of youth', has become increasingly politicised, regularly ending in scandals, public scenes or even bloodshed, as at Mexico and Munich.

(NOK), the German Olympic Society (DOG), the Games Organisation Committee (OK), the German Sports Association (DSB),
the German Sports Aid Association (DSH) and a series of industrial and banking groups. By taking part in the financing of the
Games, capital was seeking an institutional investment structure.
Thus, as Prokop goes on to point out, trusts such as Mercedes,
Coca-Cola, Flick, BMW, the Dresdner Bank, Stern magazine and
the like were actively involved through the 'German Sports Aid
Association'. German industry participated without restriction in
the financing of German sport. As of August 1972, industrial and
commercial firms had provided aid and subsidies to the tune of
30 million marks. The Games Organisation Comittee involved
representatives of the banks, insurance companies, local and national industries, the city of Munich and the Bavarian state, the
press, the churches, tourist associations, cultural and leisure organisations and so on. Thus these Games provide us with a para-
digm of a bloc of powerful interests operating as an organic totality, in this case to promote German capital and national prestige.

The publicity side of this bloc's activities drew on considerable
capital resources and ingenuity to promote national sport. Thus,
for example, the German Sports Aid Association launched a fund
drive with the slogan: 'German sport needs your help!'

'Victorious sportsmen', said an advertisement in *Speigel*, 'are
good models. Energy, perseverance, endurance, self-discipline and
sportsmanship are preconditions for sporting success . . . But these
days talent alone is not enough. To achieve the summits of performance requires preparation and training over a period of years.
So someone who has to work or study during the day has no
chance of ultimate success. Someone who cannot keep up his
training continuously because of professional commitments will
never be among the select few that make up the élite. Someone
who has to travel 50 kilometres to get to the nearest swimming
pool cannot fully devote himself to achieving major victories.
To solve these problems costs money. And that's just what our
future sportsmen lack. There's no lack of talent: your help will
bring greater success! The German sports aid foundation encourages the full development of talent and the production of
élite sportsmen. Your contribution will mean that a runner who
has to go to a training centre will no longer have to worry about

the break in his professional activity; or that a swimmer who has to travel 50 kilometres to the pool can have his petrol reimbursed; or that a weightlifter gets the three steaks a day he needs. When our sportsmen take their rightful place among the medalists at Munich you too will have cause for satisfaction. Isn't that worth a few marks?'[17]

The Games turned out to be an important boost for German capitalism and the efforts made by the firms were amply rewarded by the profits made. The construction of modern sports facilities, the provision of the material, infrastructural back up and the fulfilling of contracts provided the major capitalist names with markets of value, from a publicity as well as a directly financial point of view.

At Munich, dubbed a 'temple of technical progress' by *La Presse de Tunisie*, the big firms rivalled each other's bright ideas for promoting their latest wares and for landing building contracts. The construction of the roof of the main Olympic stadium in translucent plastic, already nick-named the biggest big top in the world, cost between 80 and 100 million marks and provided the groups which landed the contract with a favourable opening on the market and considerable advertising prestige. Needless to say the promoters engaged in tough competition for the contracts. Similarly, the electronic equipment installed to facilitate the immediate, world-wide broadcasting of the results of the events was a source of substantial profits for the big German firms. The extraordinary lengths to which the Munich organisers went in the field of sports news was a boon for the capitalist expansion of the electronics industry. It is difficult to imagine the scale of the electronic communications complex installed for the Games. Beneath the stands in the Olympic stadium was a network of 100 kilo-

17. Besides the work of Prokop, already mentioned, the following works provide further details of the economic, political and ideological mobilisation of the German Federal Republic for the Munich Games: H. H. Henschen and R. Wetter, *Anti-Olympia, Ein Beitrag zur mutwilligen Diffamierung und offentlichen Destruktion der Olympischen Spiele und anderer Narreteien*, Reihe Hanser 94, Carl Hanser Verlag, Munich, 1972; *Die vertrimmte Nation, oder Sport in rechter Gesellschaft* (a collection of articles edited by J. Richter), Rohwohlt Taschenbuch Verlag, Reinbek bei Hamburg, 1972; *Sport in der Klassengesellschaft* (a collection of articles edited by G. Vinnai), Fischer Taschenbuch Verlag, Frankfurt, 1972.

metres of cable and wiring. The five computers at the organisers' disposition were linked by 15,000 kilometres of circuitry to 400 teleprinters, 50 telex printers and 100 screens installed round the sports grounds, in the press centres and in the news offices. Olympic 'World-vision' called for a large number of video-recorders and other equipment. 60 special machines were supplied costing 500,000 marks a piece. Clearly such a concentration of advanced technology was a major source of profits for the monopolies. *La Presse de Tunisie* summed up the situation:

'The well known German electronics firms, eager for publicity, have buckled down to the task on an ambitious scale using the most sophisticated equipment . . . Munich will be a temple of technical progress. Of course, all this costs money. The biggest German firms will provide most of the installations required and about 65 million marks will be spent on them.'[18]

In this context it is easy to imagine how important it is for big capitalist firms, involved in fierce technological and financial competition, to obtain orders on this scale. In the framework of state monopoly capitalism, the big trusts are engaged in a life and death struggle for domination of the market and they do not hesitate to throw all their resources into the race after sports contracts. The *huge scale* of the Games thus gives big monopolies the chance to make *considerable* capitalist super-profits. The constant expansion of the Olympics reflects strong pressure from international capital which has everything to gain from the resulting escalation. The grotesque size of the Games, politically motivated for reasons of national prestige, is a direct expression of the tendency towards the centralisation, concentration and enlarged accumulation of capital. Consequently, the history of the Games is that of a steady escalation, from Rome, to Tokyo, from Mexico to Munich and soon to Montreal.

The other main way through which investment in the infrastructure of sport contributes to capitalist rationalisation concerns general urban development policy and, in particular, the modernisation of the facilities of large cities. The staging of the Games provides major cities with an opportunity to release resources for their own facilities. The cities concerned not only attract the

18. *La Presse de Tunisie*, 5.8.71.

capital necessary for funding investment in regional economic development, they also take advantage of the provision of sports facilities to rationalise their own growth. Thus the Munich city council grasped the opportunity provided by the Games to plan the recovery of profits on their own investment decisions. The Olympic stadium, the multi-purpose sports centre, the five-pool swimming baths, the gymnasium, the cycling track, the riding stadium, the community sports and training grounds, the Olympic village, the radio and television centre, the press centre, the railway station and underground stations, the telecommunications tower, the artificial lake, the open-air theatre, the car parks and numerous roads together with a host of other urban facilities constituted a considerable financial investment. The cost has been estimated at 1 billion, 445 million marks (£365 million), which has to be added to organisation costs of nearly 3 billion marks (£750 million).

Clearly these sums represent long term investments and the organisers have no doubt as to their eventual profitability. They have helped to speed up the capitalist modernisation of the Bavarian capital city, advantageous from two points of view. Firstly, the investments provided the city straight away with the material infrastructure needed for its efficient functioning. Secondly, they opened up the possibility of attracting capital for post-Olympic economic investment. F. Simon noted that three-quarters of these investments would in any case have been necessary sooner or later:

'Munich lacked a stadium capable of seating 80,000 people and a cycling stadium always comes in useful. As for the underground system, every city dreams of having one and Munich would certainly have had to develop its transport system in the next decade. The new motorways had been planned for years . . . In short the Olympics enabled the Bavarian capital to jump ten years ahead in its development programme, and at less expense. For, since the Games were considered a matter of national interest, the federal state undertook 50 per cent of the investments and the Bavarian state financed another 25 per cent, leaving only a quarter of the bill to be met by the city itself. . . . The facilities will be put to good use after the Games. The stadium will be used for the 1974 World Cup Finals, the bungalows of the Olympic village will become university residences and the blocks of flats will be inhabited, indeed 60 per cent of them are already sold.'[19]

In conclusion, at present there is a tendency for a small number of big trusts and monopolies to consolidate all the sports markets under their industrial and financial domination. National and international sport is itself being reduced to a part of the mechanism of state monopoly capitalism and multi-national financial groups. Contemporary sport, including, indeed especially, 'pure' Olympic sport, is entirely integrated into world capitalism. As P. Laguillaumie correctly observes: 'World sport is part and parcel of capitalist world economic strategy.'[20]

4. Towards a Capitalist Sports Industry

While the national and international sports system is rapidly being colonised by state monopoly capitalism, the capitalist groups have in their turn developed a veritable sports industry, based not only on the production of articles and commodities linked to the practice of sport, but also the provision of sports services. *The sports system has thus given rise to its own industry on a capitalist basis.* The capitalist system, as we know, obeys the laws of the expansion of capital. In order to maintain the average rate of profit in the face of inter-capitalist competition, owners of capital seek virgin areas for investment and the extraction of surplus value. The constant equalisation of the rate of profit explains the dizzy slide of capital from one sector of economic activity to another and the opening up of new areas for the accumulation of capital. This bears out the basic law of capital as Marx stated it: 'Accumulate, for ever accumulate!' To meet the difficulties caused by over-capitalisation and over-production in traditional industrial sectors, capital is invested in 'marginal' sectors such as services, tourism and sport. This explains the sudden expansion of the sports industry during the 1960s. Eventually, through a promo-

---

19. *Le Monde,* 5.4.71.
20. P. Laguillaumie, 'Pour une critique fondamentale du sport', in *Partisans, Sport, culture et répression,* Maspéro, Paris, 1968, p. 40.

tional sales strategy, the sports industry finds its way into every part of the food, clothing and leisure industries. As H. Lucot notes: 'The need for sports clothes and equipment has created a new market.'[21] This fast growing sports consumer market has rapidly been taken over by the sports product industry. And as Bonet observes: 'In the domain of sport, specialised factories and shops are mushrooming, following the development of sport itself, attracting the attention of banks and other potential investors.'[22] The production and consumption of sports shoes, tennis rackets, skis, sports bags, track-suits, balls, swimming costumes, racing bicycles, etc., has been constantly expanding, giving rise to impressive turnovers.[23] The companies concerned are not slow to launch ideological campaigns to maintain and stimulate public demand for sports articles – 'Sport for all' – 'Champion X wears Y shoes, hence his success', and so on. Just think of how certain makes of sportswear have become the favourite leisure wear of young managers and office workers.

One of the most characteristic aspects of the new sports industry which is tending to become a new sector of the economy, is the rapid expansion of sporting leisure services. With the advent of the 'leisure civilisation' or at least with the extension of paid annual holidays and mass tourism, the holiday industry and the commercial organisation of leisure activities have developed rapidly. 'Holiday producers', to borrow P. Laguillaumie's expression, have sprung up everywhere. Profiting from the advertising possibilities offered by the growing urge to get away from it all and indulge in physical activity, the capitalist trusts and the big banks have created a new market for physical leisure pursuits involving large scale financial and property deals. They have moved in to set up the necessary material and organisational infrastructure and produce the commodities and services required for sport and open air recreation. As the Communist Party programme points out: 'Skiing holidays, holidays by the sea, "exotic" holidays

21. H. Lucot, *le Sport, faut-il des surhommes?* Hachette, Paris, 1967, p. 43.
22. M. Bouet, *Signification du sport*, Editions Universitaires, Paris, 1968, p. 607.
23. As long ago as 1966, J. Meynaud observed that the sports equipment market 'had expanded rapidly. In France between 1950 and 1963, total consumption of goods and services for recreational purposes was multiplied in real terms by 1.8, and of camping and sports equipment, by 4.5.' (Op. cit. p. 41.)

136

and tourist and sporting outings are now so many commodities offered by an ever growing number of specialised agencies. Holidays are sold on credit and new resorts are launched on the market like new brands of washing powder.'[24] Already holiday credit cards are on issue. . . .

So sporting activity has given finance capital the opportunity to amass considerable profits by investing in hitherto virgin territory. For example, J. Meynaud has called attention to the 'profit possibilities involved in the fitting out of new holiday resorts, particularly ski resorts. For several years now', he adds, 'finance capital has take a special interest in the exploitation of what some commentators refer to as "white gold" '.[25] He cites the example of the creation by Rothschilds, the Suez Company and a major bank, of the Company for the Financing of Tourist Industries, involved primarily in the development of the Chamonix valley. We have already seen in the case of the Grenoble Olympics, how financial pressure groups influence the development of sports sites. But the phenomenon is a general one. The development and exploitation of recreation areas is entirely controlled by financial groups through the purchase of miles of beaches, the colonisation of natural areas by merchant banks, the commercialisation of sports centres on a huge scale, the setting up of luxury ski resorts, holiday villages, specially equipped beaches and so on. The monopolies of the sports leisure industry are merely the extensions of the big capitalist trusts. A good example is the holiday organisation, the 'Club Méditerranée', which is a complicated financial set up involving the collaboration of several different travel and tourist firms.

Conclusion

Looking at the quantity of economic data we have briefly treated, in itself by no means exhaustive, we cannot avoid the conclusion that, in the last analysis, contemporary sport is nothing but an auxiliary structure of imperialist finance capitalism, the 'final stage' of capitalism whether on a national, international or multinational level. Capital has penetrated the organisation and running of competitive sport *from top to bottom*. Sport has thereby be-

24. 'Le Parti communiste français et les activités sportives et physiques,' in *l'Ecole et la Nation*, No. 180, June 1969, p. 22.
25. J. Meynaud, Op. cit. p. 28.

come transformed into *a new type of industrial sector*, completely integrated with the other sectors of the capitalist economy. The sports system in general and the Olympic movement in particular are now an essential transmission belt in the mechanism of state monopoly capitalism. A number of theoretical and political consequences flow from this conclusion.

(i)   The primary aim of the organisers of sports or Olympic competitions is not sport for its own sake but sport for capitalist profit; or rather, their aim is capitalist profit through sport. In other words, contrary to the naïve reformist view, it is impossible to separate sporting activity proper – *pure* sport as it were (the coming together of athletes from different countries sharing the same Olympic ideal: '*citius, altius, fortius*') – from its capitalist, or at the international level, imperialist material base.

(ii)   As an element of international capitalism and the capitalist market, the institution of sport is affected by all the political upheavals, the diplomatic and military confrontations, the national antagonisms and class struggles which characterise the epoch of imperialist decay and state monopoly capitalism.

(iii)   The simultaneous and combined crisis of imperialism and Stalinism, which is today a generalised crisis of all the different levels, institutions and values of society, is hitting the world sports system and the Olympic movement head on. Sport is affected by inflation, the crisis of the international monetary system, diplomatic twists and turns, shifts in the international relationship of forces and so on. Sport in this respect confirms the general marxist proposition that the political is a concentration of the economic. Thus any objective analysis of the '*sports economy*' necessarily leads to taking a political position.

Paraphrasing Marx we can say that, 'In its rational form [the theoretical analysis of sport] is a scandal and an abomination to the bourgeoisie and its doctrinaire spokesmen, because it includes in its positive understanding of what exists a simultaneous recognition of its negation, its inevitable destruction; because it regards every historically developed form as being in a fluid state, in motion, and therefore grasps its transient aspect as well; and because it does not let itself be impressed by anything, being in its very essence critical and revolutionary.'[26]

Jean-Marie BROHM, April 1973.

26. K. Marx, *Capital* Vol. I, *Postface*, Penguin Books, London 1976, p. 103.

Towards an Institutional Analysis of Competitive Sport*

These fragmentary notes are intended simply to put forward some ideas about sport as an institution. Sport exemplifies perfectly Goffman's definition of a totalitarian totality. But unlike other institutions of capitalist society, particularly those that have often come to be called 'ideological state apparatuses' – school, church, asylum, prison, university, etc. – which have been subjected to institutional analysis, sport seems to have been completely neglected.

Sport: the Minerva's bird of institutional analysis

During the 'institutional scare' which gripped the social fabric in May '68 and in the period that followed, sport was not shaken by the kind of analytical storms which swept through the universities, the arts, medicine or psychiatry, to mention only the areas hardest hit. There was no analytical fakir to charm sport with his 'grotesque, harsh melody.'[1] A few isolated ripples reached the National Sports Institute and professional football, but these were insignificant compared with the groundswell of May '68. There were a few attempts to challenge sport – discontent in some clubs, occupations of management committees, steps towards a critique of the authoritarianism and power of federation managements by some professionals, a few moves towards unionisation in sport, etc. But these were effects of the general social climate rather

* This article appeared in *l'Homme et la Societé* (institutional and social analysis) nos. 29/30, Anthropos (July-December 1973).
  1. To paraphrase an expression used by Marx with reference to Hegelian philosophy.

than the products of contradictions internal to the institution itself.

The institution of sport is deeply tied in with a whole range of other institutions such as the army, schools, children's holiday camps, holiday clubs, prisons and so on. Sport was affected by some of the repercussions of the crisis that shook up these 'initiation institutions' as they are sometimes called. But the institutional bloc constituted by sport itself did not really develop any internal cracks. Although fringe areas of sport felt some tremors from the social earthquake, they had no lasting effects and in general the institution stood the test.

To analyse what happened in more detail, it is useful to use the distinction made in Mao's classic 1937 essay, 'On Contradiction', between internal and external contradictions. This distinction can generally be applied when analysing any kind of institution. It is important to distinguish the effect of external social contradictions on a given institution from the internal contradictions specific to the institution itself. Obviously, in the case of a generalised crisis of institutions such as developed in May '68, a dialectical combination of the two processes takes place. For example, cracks opened up in the universities due to their internal contradictions, which were in turn products of the basic contradiction between the development of the productive forces and the relations of production. And conversely, the crisis in the universities acted as an important external contradiction on a number of other institutions which were themselves weakened by their own internal contradictions. The weakest link in this chain of internal and external contradictions eventually broke, giving rise to a remarkable horizontal spreading of the social crisis throughout French institutions. One after another these institutions were hit, and the repercussions are still being felt today. To give an example, prisons and orphanages were left relatively untouched by the social crisis during May itself, but they are now going through an acute internal crisis.

While the organisational, institutional and ideological superstructure as a whole was cracked by the cumulative effect of external contradictions snowballing from one institution to the next, only a few institutions were really torn by internal conflicts.

2. Mao Tse-Tung, *On Contradiction*, Foreign Languages Press, Peking 1952.

The rest were disrupted from the outside. For instance, the student occupations of highly respectable institutions such as theatres, cinemas or protestant church halls, to hold their mass meetings, considerably jolted these institutions from the outside (and often, these occupations played a revealing analytical role). But such effects did not really constitute the outbreak of an internal crisis in the institutions concerned.

This is what happened in the case of sport. The organisational functioning of sport was disrupted, though only partially, by the general breakdown of other institutions, but the institution of sport itself remained an analytical blind-spot, an untroubled oasis in the desert of challenge to the established order. Sport was left on the sidelines, as if it were obviously to be regarded as a 'natural' institution and hence immune to criticism. In May, sport was notable for its absence. This vast institutional machine, which mobilises huge numbers of participants and spectators from all layers of society throughout the year, was subject to a sort of collective eclipse. Nobody considered sport to be relevant to the general re-examination of social institutions. Sport was repressed out of the social consciousness of the protagonists. Not only was it not analysed, it was not even considered to be open to analysis. Potential critics of sport suffered from the same sort of blindness which, according to Marx, afflicted the bourgeois economists of his time. They were so steeped in the mystified belief that the social relations and institutions on which their status was based were 'eternal and natural' rather than transitory and historical, that they were incapable of perceiving their true character.

In a period in which the political significance and the social and ideological purpose of every institution, every social relation and every social group was put into question, sport, a massive and all pervading socio-political phenomenon if ever there was one, was completely let off the hook by both theoretical and practical institutional analysis. We are here faced in a limited sense with a striking paradox of the kind which crops up from time to time in history: the blindness which leads the historical analysts to totally miss the key which would enable them to lift the famous curtain described by Hegel in the *Phenomenonology of Mind*.[3] To

3. 'It is clear then that behind the curtain as it were, which must cover the interior, there is nothing to be seen, unless *we* ourselves go behind it, both in order that there be someone to see and that there be something to be seen.' (*The Phenomenology of Mind*.)

take an example from a quite different field, during the Paris Commune, the Bank, the Stock Exchange, the Treasury and the temples to the Golden Calf at Versailles were left untouched by the insurrectionists. They thus let slip an essential lever for the institutional overthrow in which they were engaged. The communards were struck 'with holy awe before the gates of the Bank of France', as F. Engels put it.[4] They did not dare to lay a finger on this, the bourgeois fetish par excellence. Either they held it in too great a reverence, or else they simply did not see its political importance.

In a similar way, sport was not summoned to appear before the court of critical reason. The watchword which, according to René Lourau, was on everybody's lips during the May events – 'Analyse our institutions!' – was not applied to sport. So, what did happen?

The calendar of sports meetings, an essential element of the institutional mechanism of sport, was disrupted by the general strike, by the paralysis of the means of transport, the street demonstrations and disturbances and the general social climate. It was obviously difficult for public, school or college competitions to be held in this sort of situation. This disorganising influence also affected sport in the armed forces. The morale of the conscripts and the preoccupations of their officers were hardly conducive to the organisation of sports events. But by and large the institution of sport held firm, closed ranks and managed to steer clear of the breaches that were blown in the rest of the social order. On a national scale, the institutional sports concensus remained intact, and this at a time when the political class divide ran through 'civil society' in its entirety.

Not only did the institution of sport weather the storm, but it was also the first to react with the aim of restoring stability. Every effort was made to stage the major football and rugby matches as scheduled, and in particular to ensure that the national mythical epic (in the words of Barthes[5]), the Tour de France, should go ahead, giving the great annual holiday exodus of the French people a fitting send off. Who could imagine a year going

4. Introduction to *The Civil War in France*, K. Marx/F. Engels *Selected Works*, Vol. I, Lawrence & Wishart, London 1962, p. 481.
5. R. Barthes, *Mythologies*, Le Seuil, Paris 1957. [Unfortunately, *Le Tour de France comme Epopée* is not included in the selection of *Mythologies* made by J. Cape, London 1972—Ed.]

by with no Tour de France?

Meanwhile, even at the centre of the strike struggle, curious scenes could be observed. Workers occupying their factories were eager to 'kill time' by organising games of football, volley ball or pétanque. The CGT and the rest of the trade union apparatus, concerned above all to keep their members under control, organised cultural sessions and sing-songs during the occupations and urged workers to practice sport inside the factory gates rather than get involved in discussions with the students. Sport served to pass the time and divert the workers from other less harmless activities. Without interruption the sports paper l'Equipe and the other national dailies, the CP's paper l'Humanité in the lead, went on publishing reports and results. Social crises may come and go but sport goes on for ever. . . .

While young people everywhere were speaking out in the factories, the colleges and schools, the stadiums remained silent. Were young sportsmen and women really the silent majority? Certainly as far as we know, at no time were the sports grounds, swimming pools or gyms put to use as political or cultural meeting places. They remained deserted and lifeless, inhabited only by the 'negation process' eating away at society as a whole. These buildings were never used, like the National Theatre or the central university lecture halls, for open forums. Yet this was the very time when very many radicalised young people were talking about changing life-styles, rediscovering the beach beneath the paving stones, living life to the full, abolishing restrictions on pleasure, in short, thinking up a new form of bodily development in the full sense of the term – a culture in which the body would find its rightful, aesthetic, playful, erotic and intellectual place. But the very places, the ideal laboratories where this sort of practical and conceptual experimentation could have taken place, were completely ignored. Almost no attention was devoted to reflexion and criticism, directed towards giving a new status to the body within social institutions, whether in the work place or on the sports grounds. Sport still appeared as the only possible kind of relationship between man and his body. And yet, on the other hand, at a more general level the wage relation – labour power as an alienated commodity – was perceived, at least by some analysts, as something to be transcended in a society where the law of value would no longer apply. But for the collective consciousness, sport appeared to

constitute the unattainable mental horizon of our time. There
was a lot of talk *about* the body, but the body itself was not given
the chance to 'speak' in the very places supposed to be concerned
with its development. Yet just imagine the importance sports
grounds and buildings could have had for big popular gatherings
and youth festivals. The lawns and pools of the swimming baths
are ideally suited for 'utopias of the body', once the rigid control
of the sports bureaucracy is broken.

So all this time, the stadiums remained empty, waiting for
public life to return to normal to take on their usual, well regulated and institutionalised sporting functions. The emptiness of
the stadiums seems a good indication of the extent to which the
'possible consciousness' of an alternative physical practice to
that centred on competitive sport was repressed. The only relatively important incursion on to sporting terrain was the big
meeting of the left-wing parties led by Mendès-France at the
Charlety Stadium. But this had no more impact on sport as an
institution than the habitual mass meetings at the 'Palais des
Sports'.

Eventually the Tour de France took place amidst the general
respite of the French holiday period. Once the big Gaullist demonstration on the Champs-Elysées and the election victory of the
silent majority had restored law and order to the republic, public
attention could be focused on the exploits of the Tour's 'giants of
the road'. The mass media quickly passed from real social and
political conflicts to imaginary sporting jousts, duels and confrontations, and battles of every kind, concocting a sort of 'jungle
of mind and body' in which universal competition and the survival
of the fittest are sublimated through sportsmanship. The Tour
de France, like other major sports events, is a symbolic social
stage upon which good and bad, brave and bold, loyal and cunning,
mean and generous fight it out amongst themselves for the favours
of the public. The mass media put over an institutional version
of the social drama of reality, scaled down into a kaleidoscope of
collective fantasies. Political history is re-run in the hallucinatory
string of myths, identifications and ideological simplifications
which abound in the sporting press.[6] 'Our' Poulidor, France's
favourite son, the small-town hero, is indeed the idol of every

6. In his time the boxer Halimi was said to have avenged Joan of Arc
   in his fights in England!

suburbanite. The French rugby pack are a true incarnation of the vitality of the national spirit. Chauvinism on radio, television and elsewhere has never been given greater rein.

Throughout the period of social agitation and disruption a sort of institutional osmosis occurred between the language of sport and the language of real life. For instance, the press highlighted the implicit or explicit sporting aspects of confrontations between demonstrators and riot police. Terms such as 'training the troops', 'lasting the pace', 'getting second wind', 'a draw', 'neutral ground', 'the score' and 'a knock-out victory' were used. The reactionary press was unanimously of the opinion that the stone throwers would be better off putting the shot, or that the demonstrators should meet the police on the judo mat! In other words, they sought to transpose real social and political conflicts on to another stage: on to the playing field. They sought to blank out these real conflicts rather than see them actually realised via the 'patience and seriousness of the negative', which according to Hegel is the essence of the dialectic. Sportsmanship and fair play are supposed to apply in all circumstances, even those of civil war.

Such a sporting conception of politics, and of the conduct of state in general, goes hand in hand with 'political interference' in sport. Sports competition is often treated as a living metaphor for political or military reality. In a period of classic parliamentary rule, the 'terrain' is occupied by the various rival teams – the parties – who attempt to outmanoeuvre their opponents in the way a rugby pack runs round the opposing pack. Points are scored in accordance with the rules of the game. The aim is to chalk up a good electoral score, not to make your break too early so as to be pipped at the post, and so on and so forth.[7] There is a complete structural correspondence between the fields of politics and games, between sports teams and political parties with their captains or leaders, their rules of the game, their ceremonies and ideologies. Both sport and politics consist of competition between classes and social groups through the intermediary of teams or political representatives on an agreed, preferably neutral, terrain, governed by certain institutional formalities, the aim being to establish who is stronger or has majority support. While elections in France, with their eliminating rounds, are like a knock-out tournament, so

7. An expression which is often employed with respect to the Common Programme of the Union of the Left, for example.

sports competitions are a symbolic reflection of the institutional conventions of parliamentary battles, or negotiations between unions and employers.

The Mexico Olympics, held in the late summer of 1968, were a tragic confirmation of the institutional interpretation of sport and politics. Students were massacred by the national guard in the Square of the Three Cultures, Mexico City, for failing to respect the rules of the Olympic game: the truce. In Mexico, the third world was given the honour of showing the Great Powers the potential of a 'developing country' through the extravagance of the Games. The 'great festival of world youth' was from the start stained with the blood of young people protesting against military and police repression. But, in the name of 'peaceful coexistence', every country, except People's China, but including 'revolutionary' Cuba, sent their teams regardless. After all, surely the important thing is to take part! So for a while the Olympic roundabout turned at full swing. May the best man win! That's the way to prove the superiority of the 'American way of life', 'Goulash communism' or the cybernetic socialism of E. Germany. Only the black American sprinters, Carlos and Smith, with their black power salute, breached the Olympic concensus, making a first tentative step towards a critique of the institution from the inside.

In France and elsewhere, sociologists and educationalists, worried about the crisis of youth, were coming up with a prescription: if only young people were a bit more interested in sport they would get less mixed up in politics and opposition to the establishment. M. Nungesser, during his brief period as Minister for Youth and Sport in '68, echoed the views of *l'Equipe* and the majority of specialists in regarding sport as the ideal antidote to drug taking, subversion and discontent among young people.[8] 'What young people need is sport'.[9] This was the rallying cry of a frightened bourgeoisie.

There followed a series of campaigns in favour of the practice

8. 'The problems of youth and sport are closely linked, in that youth has to find an outlet in sport' (Nungesser).
9. 'Sport is a catalyst of physical and moral health and an exemplary value as far as competition goes, winning an enthusiastic public following and encouraging our young people to identify with the champions on the track, in the swimming pool and on the mountain slopes'. (ibid.).

of sport in colleges, work places and youth organisations, plans for reforming sport in France, schemes for reorganising school sport, a huge increase in sports programmes on television and so on. Sport even became an important issue in the political arena, each party claiming to be the best defender of sport. The PCF and the CGT [The Confédération Générale du Travail, the largest TU Federation in France – generally regarded as being controlled by the French CP.—Ed.] were soon to draft the Common Programme in which sport was accorded an important place. With working sportsmen, potentially recruitable to the CGT and sporting workers, the basis would be laid for making France into a 'great sporting nation', under the 'advanced democracy' of the future.

Thus the institution of sport, this great deaf-mute, not only proved the strength of its institutional base by stubbornly resisting the efforts of the old mole of analysis, but even served as a protective shield for a series of other threatened or shaky institutions. The institutionalised practice of sport served explicitly as ideological cement in the struggle to patch up the 'nation's morale' and prevent the 'collapse of morality'. Sport was promoted to the rank of saviour of other institutions. Everyone from the president down was, or soon became, a keen sportsman and friend of sport. Sport was the new darling of the republic. The state apparatus as a whole benefited from the support it received from the institution of sport, and in turn helped to stiffen sport's organisational and ideological backbone. This respectable and respected institution was considered above analytical suspicion. It was about the only one to come out of the fierce fray of May-June '68 virtually unscathed.

None of the protagonists or analysts really exposed the ideological saturation of the institution, its conservative political role and its function in structuring young people's impulses. All the various opiates of the people were subject to analysis except this one. Yet at the very beginning of the events, Youth Minister Misoffe's famous reply to Cohn-Bendit – 'If you've got sexual problems, take a dip in the pool' – could have been the starting point for such an analysis. This reply, sums up, better than any theoretical proposition, one of the essential aspects of the institution: *libidinal repression*. But although the Nanterre students were the first to highlight the institutionalisation of sexual repression, they completely neglected sport as a potential new field for criticism. They were the first to analyse a whose series of institutions but they unconsciously let sport slip by. The only trace left by the events which in any sense compensated for the absence of a sociology of sport forged in the heat of action, was the production of a few pamphlets, including an issue of the review, *Partisans: Sport, culture et répression*.[10] The Minerva's bird of institutional analysis took to flight only belatedly and without much sporting conviction.

Challenging the Institution of Sport

However, the analysts' slumber did not last much longer. The institution of sport began to move under the indirect effects of the general challenge to society and its institutions that followed the May events.

The Munich Olympics were proof enough that sport was ripe for institutional analysis. These Olympics were not only affected internally by the latter; they also had a considerable impact in the field of politics. More clearly than any other event, they revealed the true nature of the international social and political relationships concealed beneath the smokescreen of 'peaceful coexistence'. This is not the place to describe the institutional process played out in the tragic theatre of Munich throughout the Games.[11] We will merely examine a few typical examples which bring out the main stages in the outbreak of critical analysis.

The entire series of events at the Games can be interpreted as a sequence of freudian slips, repressed drives, symptoms and 'actings out'. Munich was an immense institutional flop, which demonstrated that the repression of drives can have a boomerang effect. The endless incidents, excesses, hesitations and fumblings, and the prevalent mood of guilt, bad conscience and unease were all signs that the institution of sport had gone into a deep crisis.

---

10. Republished in paperback edition – Maspéro, 1972, at the time of the Munich Games. Attention should also be drawn to the relevant remarks on sport in G. Lapassade, *Procès de l'Université, institution de classe*, Belfond, Paris, 1969.
11. Cf. articles in *le Chrono Enrayé*.

Munich: One Tragedy Follows Another

The very choice of site for the Olympics is proof of both a repression of the recent past and at the same time a determination to exorcise and de-dramatise it. The Games were staged on the very spot where the statesmen of Europe had met to sign the famous Munich agreement which had given the signal for the advance of Nazi barbarity which followed. Moreover the site was not far from Dachau, the principle scene of the genocidal exploits of the 'master race' (who were already highly sporting at the time). The explicit intention was to 'wipe the slate clean'. Unofficial expiation ceremonies were held at Dachau and elsewhere before the opening of the Games. Willy Brandt's social democratic government was seeking to put over a different image of Germany from that presented when last the Games had been staged in Germany, in Berlin in 1936. The Nobel peace prize winner hoped to take advantage of Munich to mark Germany's definitive admission into the 'family of great civilised nations'. The Olympic truce, explicitly founded on the renunciation of the Hitlerite past, also expressed the will, or rather the illusion, of defending peace amongst men. The peace of the Olympics was held to promote universal brotherhood, the celebration of youth, and friendship between peoples and races, at least within the Olympic village. The General Secretary of the UN, Kurt Waldheim, declared: 'The Olympic Games represent one of the earliest and most noble of mankind's attempts to promote friendship, understanding and reconciliation between the peoples of the entire world.' Meanwhile American imperialism went on with its massive bombing of Indochina, the Palestinian resistance was hunted down and persecuted by Zionism and Arab reaction and the peoples of Latin America suffered bloody repression at the hands of military dictatorships.

So from an institutional point of view, the Games had, from the start, the function of repressing the political conflicts of the real world into the subconscious. *l'Equipe*'s editorialist, describing Munich as the 'centre of the world', regarded the Games not just as a way of forgetting international political and military conflicts but also as a means of establishing an oasis of peace in the midst of 'a world gone made' (as another paper put it). Munich, as an example of peaceful coexistence, of the truce and of peace, was, above all, a vast illusion machine, salving consciences, encouraging complacent hypocrisy and glorifying the established order. Olympic sport was held to be above struggles between states and classes: a transcendent, almost mystical phenomenon whose 'prime virtue was to establish peace between men and nations', in the words of J. Goddet, editor of *l'Equipe* (26.8.72). More modestly, *France Soir* expressed the wish that the political role of the Games would be to 'enable people, for a few days at least, to forget the internecine wars which plague our time of pseudo-peace, from Korea to Vietnam, from Algeria to Angola and from Bangladesh to the Middle-East' (7.9.72). In short, the Olympic concensus was based on an attempt to erase political reality from people's minds, substituting the fiction of peace and the illusion of a truce. Given that the Games operate in this way as a sort of blind spot, it was inevitable that they would sooner or later be invaded by politics, which in the words of *France Soir* (7.9.72), 'had long been besieging the walls of the Olympics.' Throughout the Games a series of political intrusions occurred, either through demonstrations, meetings or debates, arising from issues such as racist Rhodesia, the Irish war or Vietnam.

But the true *historical analyst* of the Games was the *Black September* commando. Their violent, premeditated 'acting out' brought to light both the mechanisms and structures and the social bases of the Olympic institution. Setting aside the question of whether or not their action was effective or politically correct, which is the subject of another debate altogether, for the moment *we are concerned with grasping the analytical effects their action had on an unprecedented scale.*

At the general political level, which is not our immediate concern, Black September's action brought about a particularly clear political realignment, putting everybody on the spot. Every capital city had to make its attitude clear. These ranged from the silence, embarrassment or condemnation expressed by the 'friends of the Palestinian resistance', China, the USSR, E. Germany, Egypt *et al.*, to the unanimous protest from the big Western powers in condemnation of this 'barbarity'. Indeed the light shed by the Munich events on real political relationships was as revealing as social democracy's betrayal in August 1914. In both cases the veil was lifted. *Hic Rhodus, hic salta!*

At the level of the Olympic institution itself, Black September's action *brought out with striking clarity* all the political, economic, ideological and symbolic factors which structure sport. The idealist, mythical, conservative Olympic ideology suffered a heavy blow. Suddenly the prevailing massive *false consciousness* was blown open. The commando's action was intended as a demonstration, in the heart of the Olympic village, that 'peaceful coexistence', the truce, the Olympic peace and the rest were mere ideological masks for the holy alliance of the great powers against the small, for the coalition of the oppressors against the oppressed and for the pact between ruling classes against oppressed people and classes. The *unanimous,* virtually identical, reaction of all governments, international agencies and institutions, ranging from the Vatican and the UN to the International Olympic Committee, was a clear indication that Olympic ideology had gone by the board. The Olympic peace was compatible with the slaughter of thousands of victims in Indochina or with massacres in Latin America and Africa,[12] but Black September's *transgression of the mythical symbolism of the institution was too much.*[13]

'The assassination of a myth', was *le Figaro*'s headline (6.9.72). 'The death of an ideal', wrote the *Parisien Libéré* on the same day. Jaques Goddet, writing in *l'Equipe* (6.9.72), summed up the general reaction: 'Such an attack on one of the most generous ideas produced by the 20th Century, all too familiar with disasters and tragic divisions, this attack on the Olympic ideal, the fraternal gathering of the élite of world youth, seems to me to be an additional crime, equally to be condemned.' This reaction was little different from that of *France Nouvelle,* organ of the PCF (12.9.72). For them the action was 'a blow to the strengthening of the Olympic ideal'. As R. Cartier stressed in *Paris Match,* the Palestinians' real crime was to have 'breached the Olympic peace'. They had dared to violate an ideology, to destroy the Olympic ideal, to break with the universal concensus. Cartier went on, 'Despite their divergent social systems, the Olympic nations shared certain basic *ideas* and *principles.* They all more or less respected the univers-

12. In a similar way the 1936 Berlin Olympics, the apotheosis of the Hitler régime, involved the *de facto* if not the *de jure* acceptance of the barbaric nazi war machine. By accepting to take part in the Berlin Games, the high-flown universal conscience was accepting the 'final solution', the camps, fascist totalitarianism and the invasion of Europe by the SS hordes.
13. Whatever one may think of the means employed by the commando, which were obviously highly questionable.

alist and humanist principles behind the Games. *The Olympics were based on an accord between civilised men. This barbaric invasion is a threat to the future of the Games.'*

The violence of the reactions to Black September's action indicated the *opaque character of Olympic ideology*. The analytical effect of the action consisted in the practical demonstration that Olympic ideology is a highly organised reactive system whose power is in direct proportion to the strength of the drive it seeks to repress, namely politics and the struggle between classes and states, Olympic ideology, expressed in terms of *ultra-pacificist values*, axioms, attitudes and opinions, is a permanent counterweight to and mask of the formidable institutionalised weight of *aggression*, competition, struggle, war and in the final analysis, death. The desperate obsession with the rigid ideology reflected in an entire range of ceremonies[14] and rituals of peace-making, brotherhood and universal tolerance, is really a defence mechanism, a sort of Maginot line against the ever-present, latent intrusion of hatred and conflict. The litanical, hectoring and sermonising tone of Olympic language is a strong sign of the defensive function of its underlying ideology. The orchestrated repetition of the humanist themes of this ideology betrays the inhumanity lurking just below the surface of a world which needs to stage regularly this extravaganza of bodies, kind hearts and good intentions.

The very statesmen, officials and personalities who before the commando raid were vaunting universalist, humanitarian or even 'internationalist' sentiments, now launched into the attack on the savagery of the 'new barbarians' and closed ranks in defence of 'Western civilisation'. Their imperialist chauvinism, racism and xenophobia was given free rein. What was supposed to be a ritual expiation for the racist and anti-semitic crimes committed in the past by German fascism became the scene of an unprecedented flood of anti-Arab and anti-Palestinian racism. The ideologists and organisers of the Olympic movement, led by Mr. Brundage, who up to then had been singing the praises of 'brotherhood-between-all-men-of-whatever-race-colour-or-creed', now joined in

14. In fact, the grotesque and comic ceremonials of the Olympics combine in a sort of 'compromise formula', symbols of peace – doves, the oath, the Olympic emblem etc. – and military-style rites – march pasts, flag ceremonies, national anthems, medal ceremonies, the lighting of the torch etc.

the hysterical campaign against the Palestinians, treating them as fanatics and pariahs of the human community, reminding one of the time when the Olympic movement closed its eyes to the anti-semitism of the 'new Aryans', or more recently, when it covered up for racism in South Africa and Rhodesia.

The 'neutral' Olympic ideology served as a cover for an operation of banishment, exclusion and persecution against the Palestinians and provided the pretext for a violent, spontaneous epidemic of racism in the Bavarian capital. Victor Cygielman of *le Nouvel Observateur* (11.9.72), described the new climate reigning in the 'temple of peace' in the following terms:

> 'So far the term *"Untermenschen"* (sub-humans) is not being used, but on a banner raised by demonstrators against the raid on Wednesday evening was written, "Are these people human?". "No Arabs" signs are appearing in cafés. In the nearby Volkswagen factory, on Wednesday morning, the North-African workers had to be "parked" out of harm's way. Anti-Arab sentiment is the predominant reaction. *People have quickly passed from humanitarian sentiments to a strangely transformed racism.* Now, the dark-skinned, hook-nosed individual depicted in *Bild* is no longer the Jew of Goebbel's *Völkischer Beobachter* but an Arab (a Palestinian? nobody here bothers to make the distinction) holding hostage five Israelis in chains.'

By tearing open the veil at its weak-point, the Palestinians exploded Olympic ideology. Once a crack had been opened in the armoured protective shield of the institution of sport, a great *cathartic reaction* was set loose. The violence of this reaction demonstrates the extent to which the drives had been repressed. By highlighting the duplicity and hypocrisy of the Olympic ideology, the Palestinians brought out the 'self-deception' – the denial of reality – underlying international sport, one of the last pillars of the established order hitherto untouched. This explains the unprecedented resort to the institution's repressive and ideological defence mechanisms. (All analysis gives rise to resistance.) 'We are outraged and horrified by the Munich raid which besides its obvious cowardice, is really a double crime: first and foremost against humanity, but also against one of the *last noble and generous ideals* left in this world of violence – the Olympic ideal.' This passage from *l'Aurore* is a good example of the double ignorance on which the ideology of Olympic sport is founded: ignorance of the concrete conditions determining social relations between classes, as expressed in the use of the term 'humanity' with a capital 'H', and ignorance of the true origins and the illusory character of the Olympic ideal. Thus the language of abstractions succeeds in turning reality upside down, as Marx had observed.[15]

Clearly, in analysing this ignorance, the Palestinians were certain to bring down the wrath of the clique of ideologues. And by disrupting the ideological establishment, the analysts also brought out the material, political and economic determinants underlying the institution. We cannot develop this analysis in detail here, but we will take a few examples.

The huge police and army operation launched at Munich to deal with the fanatics revealed, though only after the event, the meaning of the permanent saturation of the Olympic village with security forces. The great festival of youth looked more like a massive gathering of police and secret service agents come to protect the 'peaceful' contests. The response of the Bavarian security forces revealed the cooperation that existed all along between the police, the army and German and foreign secret services. The formidable deployment of *Wehrmachte* forces, the marksmen of the *Bundesgrenschutz*, the police-dogs, machine-guns and special 'anti-guerrilla' units were evidence that the 'haven of peace', the Olympic village, was in good hands. The athletes were more or less under house arrest, surrounded by helicopters, armoured cars and black and green uniforms. In Berlin, at least things had been clear, even if observers closed their eyes to what was going on. In 1936, the high mass of the Olympic religion was celebrated under the 'protection' of the Hitler Youth, the SS and the nazi goon squads parading in a sea of fascist banners, flags and emblems. At Munich, security obviously had to be more 'democratic'. The police surrounding the sports facilities donned track suits appropriate to 'sporting stewards'. The strong-arm

---

15. 'If in all ideology men and their relations appear upside down as in a *camera obscura*, this phenomenon rises from their historical life-process (. . .) The phantoms formed in the brains of men are also, necessarily, sublimates of their material life-process.' K. Marx and F. Engels, *The German Ideology*, in K. Marx/F. Engels *Collected Works*, Vol. 5, Lawrence & Wishart, London 1975, p. 36.

men were dressed up as holiday camp leaders.

Continuing to unravel the analytic thread, it was also possible, *after the event*,[16] to grasp the meaning of a number of apparently insignificant facts which were completely trivialised by the mass media. The *all pervading* presence of the military and police apparatus suddenly became visible. The Socialist Party newspaper *l'Unité* wrote:

> 'The army is everywhere – during the opening ceremony a German policeman was the last to bear the torch.' Roland Faure in *l'Aurore* (25.8.72) described the situation as follows: 'One German soldier carried my luggage up to my room, another ran my bath and cleaned the bathroom, yet another provides room service and brings me coffee in the mornings and refreshments during the day. . . . Amongst all the publicity operations that have thrived during these Olympics, the campaign in favour of the *Bundeswehr* has undoubtedly been the most spectacular and the least expected. This 25,000 strong force, mobilised for the most peaceful of purposes, provides a reassuring image – the more so for the fact that I write from one end of a street with the particularly evocative name of Dachau . . .'.

25,000 men, not counting the police and other special units . . . A journalist thus innocently reveals *the colossal presence of the state's repressive apparatus.*

Following the trail a little further, we learn that 'for one well known team, 18 gendarmes disguised as sportsmen are acting as chauffeurs.' (F. Simon, *Le Monde* 2.9.72.) We learn that most of the national teams included a good number of soldiers, policemen, gendarmes, customs officers, trainee officers and security agents; that the administrative and organisational members of the teams included a fair proportion of 'special' officials – 'interpreters' in the case of E. European countries – 'chaperones' or 'security officials' in other cases. It became increasingly clear that the Games had all the appearance of a confrontation of 'armed propaganda', to use an expression of North Vietnamese theoreticians. Elite sports battalions went to the Olympic front, well armed with the necessary service corps. The representatives of the state, the spokesmen of the nation, doubled as *little soldiers on duty* in the stadiums, defending national prestige and the national flag

16. In the Freudian sense of the term.

in their own special way. The welding together of the institutions of sport and the army thus became clear to see. The Israeli delegation provided a good example of the 'spartan' composition of the teams, some of which functioned rather like fortified camps (notably E. Germany).

By breaking down the general mechanisms by which sport is regimented, the analysts also made it possible to 'read' or 'decypher' phenomena usually classified as anecdotal incidents, and to understand how they related to the institutional system. These incidents were symptomatic of general repression in sport, reflected in its authoritarianism, its bureaucracy and particularly its *moral order*. This moral order appeared in very concrete form, in blatant contradiction with the ideological affirmation of the freedom, sense of responsibility and maturity of the athletes. We learned, for example, that the Olympic village was organised like a huge convent, with a formal separation of the dormitories by an 'anti-flirting fence', manned by guardians of the athletes' morals. *l'Equipe* carried the following description of this boarding school set up:

> 'The anti-flirting fence separating the boys from the girls, like a "wall of shame" running through the Olympic village, is still an endless topic of conversation. No other initiative has been so controversial . . . Only a few holes (sic) have been opened here and there for service purposes, but they are barred by strapping lads in light blue uniforms like so many Cerberuses guarding the gates of hell.' (*l'Equipe* 30.8.72.)

We also learned that the 'American team managers, who don't take discipline lightly, have posted a list of rules for their team members in the entrance hall. The tone of these rules must be a little over strict, because some wag has signed the notice "Adolf Hitler" '. (*l'Equipe* 25.8.72.) In short the Olympic village, run on the lines of a scout jamboree, took every possible precaution against the threat of disturbances, immorality or 'bodily contact', resorting to the traditional recipes for the purpose: early to bed; no excesses; don't get tired; be serious; and so on. The manager of French athletics, R. Bobin, gave his team the following warning:

> 'I want you to be noticed on the track, but not in the village. You shouldn't need me to tell you that you have made too many

sacrifices to spoil everything by fooling around here. You will have to go to bed early, without disturbing the others. We will be very strict. The first one to play the fool will be put on the first plane back to Paris. This isn't a holiday you know.' (*Le Monde* 26.8.72.)

By shaking up the institution, the analytic vanguard also encouraged the intervention of other, perhaps secondary but often no less effective analysts. We will take just two eloquent examples.

One way to salute the flag!

We all know how much these great institutional bodies love official ceremonies which give them the chance to show off. Olympic ceremonial is no exception. *The organisation's rituals help to bind it together ideologically.* This explains the compulsive, obsessive character of such rituals. It also explains why any breach of the rules of the game is stigmatised as an unpardonable sin. *The observance of protocol is a basic characteristic of all such rigid ideological apparatuses.* The Black American runners, Matthews and Collett, demonstrated this fact by *ridiculing* a typical ceremony: the presentation of medals accompanied by national anthems. Following the 400 metres final, while the bronze medalist Julius Sang (from Kenya) stood rigidly to attention on the podium, the two Americans, in front of the national flags and the entire assembly of officialdom, simply adopted a casual pose, turning to each other. ostentatiously chatting, a slightly wicked smile on their lips. One even went as far as to hold his running shoes in one hand. . . . At first the silent crowd was puzzled, not realising what was going on, then began to mutter and whistle the heretics down as deviants from the ritual. Their sin was indeed grave. Suppose two soldiers on parade were to behave in the same way as the two athletes? Namely: 'showing ostentatious lack of interest during an official ceremony, intentionally ill-behaved and dressed in a manner verging on indecency'. (*Le Figaro* 8.9.72.) Their attitude even had 'the appearance of deliberate provocation', continued *France Soir* (9.9.72). This intolerable conduct was indeed not tolerated by the crowd who like nothing better than military music, parades, marches, salutes and medal ceremonies. The crowd amply and vociferously shouted them down. 'This implicit challenge to protocol,' wrote *l'Aurore* (8.9.72), 'was not particularly appreciated by the general public'. What greater scandal than to sin against fetishes, taboos and sacred values such as national anthems or Olympic medals! One of the two athletes, doubtless irritated by the howl of indignation, committed two further sins. He raised his clenched fist in salute and played with his medal as if it were a mere toy. According to *l'Equipe*'s man on the spot, 'He removed the gold medal from around his neck and casually spun it round his outstretched arm like a rattle.' Amidst general outcry, the crowd whistled still louder.

Yoo-hoo, here I am!

Another little incident had an important analytic effect. *It revealed and ridiculed the climate of voyeurism, exhibitionism and sado-masochism pervading the Games,* particularly during that quintessential trial of endurance, the Marathon. Inspired by the legendary Marathon of antiquity, it embodies the myths of self-denial, of struggle in the face of death and of the superhuman exploit. In many ways it is the crowning event of the Games and is always packed with incidents, unexpected upsets and suspense. All the great Olympic Marathons have contributed their share of epic exploits to sporting history, evoked by names like Zatopek, Mimoun, Abebe *et al.* Most such races end in more or less tragic scenes with some athletes collapsing at the finishing line, others completely 'smashed', staggering and grimacing like the 'steam train' Zatopek, or else continuing round the track, unaware that the race is finished. In other words, the marathon is the high point of the Games. It is certainly the best example of the morbid intoxication with physical pain, transfigured through effort, to the limits of human capacity, even to the risk of death, described by L. Mumford in *Technics and Civilisation.*[17]

But at the Munich Games tragedy was turned into farce. While the crowd was anxiously awaiting the entry of the leading runner

17. 'Sport, in the sense of a mass-spectacle, with death to add to the underlying excitement, comes into existence when a population has been drilled and regimented and depressed to such an extent that it needs at least a vicarious participation in difficult feats of strength or skill or heroism in order to sustain its waning life-sense (. . .) is it not fundamentally for the sake of exciting just such bloodlust that the competition itself is held and widely attended?' Lewis Mumford, *Technics and Civilisation,* G. Routledge & Sons, London, 1934, pp. 303/304.

into the Olympic stadium, expecting to see the American, Shorter, who had been ahead up to then, a 16-year-old, long-haired W. German school student, wearing white shorts and a light-blue vest marked number 72, appeared on the track, a few minutes before the arrival of the true winner. He put on a show of being tired and did a triumphal round of the track to the cheers of the crowd, and to the astonishment of the officials and security guards who had let him slip through. Meanwhile the entry of the real winner went by un-noticed. The triumphal entry of the gods was brought into ridicule. From then on people would have to think twice before applauding. Thus the grandure and pathos of the event was exploded by a mere blunder on the part of the security officials. The crowd, feeling cheated, found it difficult to start their ovation all over again with the same spontaneity. The sabotage effected by this little spanner in the formidable organisational works of the Games, with all their computers, electronic circuitry and TV channels played a double analytical role. First, it showed that the giant had feet of clay. By throwing the meticulously orchestrated sequence of events out of gear, the incident demonstrated the bureaucratic inanity of the formalism and 'prussian efficiency' of the Games' organisation. Secondly, it de-mystified the role of the champion, the haloed figure bathing in the glory of victory. What could be more humiliating and scandalous than for a winner to be deprived of his moment of triumph? 'The purpose of my act', said the young student, 'was to protest against the solemnity, seriousness and over-organisation reigning at Munich.' (*Le Monde,* 12.9.72.) At any rate, judging from the reaction of M. Hansenne of *l'Equipe,* he achieved his aim: 'This usurper of glory deprived us of those few priceless seconds when the crowd rises to acclaim the most deserved of victories. Emotion gave way to farce, with the blessing of the green-uniformed watchdogs. It will take a long time to get over our disappointment.' (*l'Equipe,* 12.9.72.)

These two natural analysts bursts into the institution like puppies disrupting a game of ninepins. Their analytic role went outside all official structures. The two American runners were the black sheep of the Olympic family, while the young student was a disruptive, provocative spanner in the works. Their interventions gave an analytic sense to the incidents, breakdowns, misunderstandings, frictions, minor conflicts and 'miss-hits' which, within the dominant, organisational, positivist mode of thought, are interpreted as mere mistakes, flaws in the system or organisational hitches of no importance for the institution. After all, no machine is perfect is it? In other words the dominant positivism can never conceive that these 'slips' are outbreaks of *negativity* in the institution, revealing contradictions and conflicts between its different elements. Instead they are conceived as mere indications that the system is not totally consistent.

To remove the effects of entropy and improve the reliability of the system, all that is needed, surely, is to rationalise, streamline and reorganise it a little. It is only to be expected that a system as thoroughly positivist as sport and the Olympic movement should be unable to conceive of the existence within itself of an analytical negativity which lays bare its structures, enabling us to interpret them. This explains why the institution defensively closes its ranks and stubbornly resists everything which *makes sense* of it or develops an analysis which challenges its legitimacy as an established order. While the institution has been able to accept some analysis *of* itself, in the form of symposiums, debates and the like, it cannot tolerate analysts *within* itself. To do so would mean accepting another, radically different logic from that which guides its normal operation. Accepting analysis means going into crisis. In the case of the Olympic institution, this meant bringing into the open the cleavages, splits, divisions and clashes between classes, states, interests, motives and ideologies which lie behind the apparently unanimous facade. This could clearly be seen in the course of the few hours when the institution was on a knife edge, uncertain of its own continued existence: to be or not to be; to continue or not to continue. For a time this tower of Babel, shaken to its very foundations, began to crack and crumble, striving to avoid complete disintegration. This confirmed once again that the analyst is a destroyer (and not just of illusions). He could be described as a new type of vandal. As R. Lourau puts it: 'The analyst, by dismantling institutionalised social relations, forces people to take sides, to put their cards on the table and to speak or act in such a way as to prove who they are and justify what they say. His effect is to bring to the surface the power relations concealed beneath the ideology of the common good and the concensus.'[18]

---

18. *Les Analyseurs de l'Eglise*, Editions Anthropos, Paris, 1972, p. 20.

Conclusion: In the Institution of Sport, the Natives are Restless

Independently of the historical and natural analysts[19] who have brought about an unprecedentedly widespread questioning of the institution, a development of both theoretical and practical criticism of competitive sport took place around the Munich Games. This critique took many different forms, ranging from the setting up of anti-Olympic committees in France, Germany and Italy, to a whole variety of anti-establishment activity.[20] In France in particular, the activity of the anti-Olympic committee met with a certain echo. *l'Humanité Dimanche*, as usual, felt obliged to put anti-Olympic agitation down to the work of 'Krivine and his friends'. When institutions are seized by the 'bacchic delirium' of the negative truth, described by Hegel in the *Phenomenology of Mind*, they resort to police conceptions of history. Unable to admit that every institution contains its own contradictions, every social crisis is attributed to plots and foreign or outside interference.

However, for some time now the most clear sighted bourgeois observers have been realising that sport's star is on the wane and that the aspiration to find a new life-style is aiding the progress of an alternative way of developing the body. The employers' journal *Les Informations* (4.9.72) rather anxiously noted the growing number of people 'fed up with sport', in an article entitled 'Is Sport Right-wing?':

'In the middle of the Olympic Games, sport is challenged. And not just by those people who have always condemned sport as a vast commercial affair. The critique goes further: not content with attacking the political use that is sometimes made of sport...

19. For these notions Cf. R. Lourau, *Situation de l'analyse institutionelle en 1972*, in *les Temps modernes*, No. 312-313, 1972.
20. For a more detailed account, besides the issue of *Partisans: sport, culture et répression*, Maspéro, 1968, previously mentioned, see the following works and pamphlets: Two special issues of *Le Chrono Enrayé* devoted to the Olympics, May 1972 and September 1972 which still constitute the most thorough-going and radical critique of the Olympics; the special dossier on the Olympics in *Politique Hebdo*, 7.9.72, entitled 'La fausse trève'; These articles draw up a detailed balance sheet of challenges to the Olympics in France and internationally. More generally: H. H. Henschen and R. Wetter, *Anti-Olympia*, Hanser, Munich, 1972; and U. Prokop, *Soziologie der olympischen Spiele, Sport und Kapitalismus*, Munich, Hanser, 1971.

the far left now condemns the very values which have been its main strengths – team-spirit, the will to win, the discipline of training. These values, they claim are simply modelled on the values of a capitalist society. Like the family, progress or hard work, sport is one of those values we thought were solid, universally accepted, politically neutral and above party quarrels. Now we find that sport in its turn has come into the rebels' line of fire. "Fed up with sport", the cry of the radical young, signifies something more: what is at stake is not only politics, but morality and civilisation itself.'

More recently, during the National Sports Week in Amiens in May 1972, which brought together sociologists, psychologists, politicians, army officers, youth leaders, sports managers and leading sportsmen, several analytical contributions made it clear that time was up for sport. Sport could no longer escape institutional analysis with its customary skilful evasive tactics. As Marx would have said, *De te fabula narratur!* – it's your story they are telling!

The *Le Monde* reporter, F. Simon realised perfectly well that reactions of resistance to analytical interference reflected, as he put it, 'the rigid defence of a threatened ideology'. He had to admit the obvious fact that the process of analytic ferment was developing independently of the subversive actions of extremist left-wingers, who, either because of intellectual complacency or ideological blindness are always cast in the role of the evil spirits – the *Deus ex Machina* plotting the downfall of the system.

'It will doubtless be said,' he went on, 'that not too much importance should be given to the exaggerated declarations of the left-wing sects who came to put over their anti-establishment message with aggressive persistence. It is true that several times rowdy youngsters disrupted the general academic atmosphere. However the somewhat hysterical reaction they aroused cannot simply be explained by the suspicion in which they are customarily held. The unease stemmed from the fact that they threw into doubt axioms which serve as permanent reference points for the world of sport. This is confirmed by the fact that the same doubts, when voiced by well known personalities, produced just the same unease, if not the same outraged reaction.' (*Le Monde*, 19.5.73.)

The fundamental challenge to competitive sport was under way, and this fact haunted the consciousness of the participants. From then on it was clear that this process of questioning could not stop half way. Amid general astonishment, a young 'left-wing extremist' provided an outline of the programme which is now on the stocks:

'I hope that there is no future for competitive sport, and that it will disappear, along with the type of society with which it is associated. I can't see the point of pushing someone into swimming up and down a pool for four or five hours at a time. We are told that this is the way to develop a sense of effort for its own sake. But what is the point of developing such a sense? We are confusing the fact of knowing how to swim with the self-fulfilment of the individual.' (*Le Monde,* 19.5.73.)

Jean-Marie BROHM, June 1973.

The Anti-Olympic Appeal of the 'Ecole Emancipée'*

At a time when the B.52s are slaughtering the Vietnamese people, the Munich Olympics will dominate the headlines. Thousands of people, fascinated by the medal ceremonies will be stirred by the rhythm of 'their' national anthems and the victories of 'their' athletes.

It is impossible to stay silent while allowing this mascarade to assume such international dimensions that it masks imperialist crimes throughout the world, particularly against the peoples of Indochina, by claiming to bring about reconciliation between all states on the sports ground.

That is why we propose to initiate an ANTI-OLYMPIC CAMPAIGN around the following themes:

(1) *The Olympic Games and Imperialism*

Major international sports competitions such as the Olympics are part and parcel of a vast sporting/commercial complex. As a source of considerable profits, the organisation of such events is the object of fierce rivalry between nations and cities. This competition is reflected at every level:

— that of the sports industry itself: sports facilities, swimming pools, ski slopes, skis etc. (eg 16 million pairs of skis sold at Sapporo);

— that of control equipment: computers, electronic timing devices etc.;

— that of the provision of facilities in the region: motorways, hotels etc.;

*This appeal first appeared in *Le Chrono Enrayé*, No. 9 (October-November 1972).

– that of the mass media: television and newspapers;

– that of advertising outlets: the fight for the most favourable advertising sites. The champions notably in the Winter Olympics become virtual sandwich-board men: official representatives of the firms which provide their equipment and finance.

At Munich in 1972 a sports/finance bloc has been set up around the jar of honey constituted by the Games, consisting of the German Olympic Committee, the German Olympic Society, the Munich Olympics Organisation Committee, the German Sports Association, and the German Sports Aid Association, set up by trusts such as Coca-Cola, Flick and BMW together with a series of industrial and banking companies. This bloc of powerful interests operates as an organic whole to promote German capital and national prestige.

The way capital has established its hold over the Olympics is a perfect example of the present tendency of sport to become state monopoly sport. By integrating sport into its economic structures, state monopoly capitalism has also turned sport into a cog in the bourgeois state machine. Sport is an important element of present day imperialist policy. In this regard, it should be noted that major sports meetings and competitions were originally established at the start of the epoch of imperialism around the turn of the century. The international organisation of sport through international federations, the IOC and so on, is linked to the institutional agencies of imperialism, particularly American imperialism: agencies such as the UN, UNESCO etc. Moreover the ideology of sport is an element of imperialist ideology. Sports activity and the Olympics have always been tied in with the political ups and downs of world diplomacy and attempts at imperialist domination:

– The Berlin Games in 1936 provided the Hilter régime with a massive propaganda platform, contributing to the consolidation of the fascist state;

– The Melbourne Games in 1956 took place at the time when French and British troops were invading the Suez canal so that the imperialist trusts could continue to dominate the Middle-East and control Middle-East oil. These Games shortly followed the bloody crushing of the workers councils in Hungary and the massacres of Budapest.

– The Mexico Games in 1968 were staged three months after the events of May and June in France, the most remarkable mass mobilisation ever seen in an advanced capitalist country. Only one month before the Games opened the stalinist tanks moved into Czechoslovakia to put down the powerful anti-bureaucratic movement. Thus, like the Olympics in Rome in 1960 and in Tokyo in 1964, the Mexico Games were one of the means of subtly bringing the class struggle back to normal. But the Mexico students made sure that this masquerade was shown up in its true colours. The Mexico Games could only be held after the massacre in the Square of the Three Cultures – and then only under the permanent armed guard of fascist Diaz Ordaz's troops.

– In 1972, diplomacy is in command.

After the bloodbath needed to crush the popular insurrection in Ceylon, the crushing of the workers' movement in the Sudan, the defeats of the Palestinian resistance and the genocide perpetrated by US imperialism in Indochina, Nixon, seeking a diplomatic solution in face of the imminent American defeat at the hands of the Indochinese revolution, is hoping to reach a deal with Moscow and Peking behind the backs of the Indochinese peoples. The 'little balls that bring friendship' (in the words of *Peking News*), the ping-pong diplomacy between the Chinese and the Americans have opened the way towards collaboration in international sport.

– The Munich Games will be an opportunity for the great powers to consolidate these diplomatic moves. For American imperialism in particular, the aim is to conceal the world class struggle and claim to be striving for happiness and brotherhood between all nations.

(2) *The Olympics and the Bureaucratic, Stalinist Bloc*

The function of the Olympics in these countries can only be understood on the basis of a political analysis of the history of betrayal of the workers' movement by the stalinist bureaucracy, especially as this has developed since 1945.

In 1945 the Yalta and Potsdam agreements set the seal on the division of the world into 'Western' and 'Communist' spheres of influence. One of the consequences of these agreements was the participation of the USSR in the creation of the United Nations, that 'brigands' cave'.

Within this class collaborationist framework, the USSR came to play an increasingly important role in the development of world sport:

- 1951: admission into the IOC.
- 1952: participation in the Helsinki Games.
- 1980: proposal that Moscow organise the Olympics.

During this time the Stalinist bureaucracy has increasingly had to sweep the international class struggle under the carpet in order to justify the 'theory' of sport as a means of promoting world peace.

According to the strategy of 'peaceful coexistence between states with different social systems', as defined by Khruschev, international sports contests, like scientific rivalry or the comparison of economic growth rates, are the arena for peaceful competition between the countries concerned.

Thus the number of medals a country wins is not just a boost for nationalism and chauvinism but is also a measure of a country's place in the international league table.

For most countries, the number of medals they win is taken as an index of the vitality of their social and political system.

On the basis of this strategy of class collaboration through sport, the French Communist Party (PCF) gives an important place to sport in its policy of union of the French people and the anti-monopoly alliance.

- The PCF takes part in the vast mystificatory operation developed by the bourgeoisie through sport, encouraging workers to identify with their Companies, which benefits only the employers.
- the party organises inter-workshop and inter-factory sports competitions. The ultimate in this line followed the great general strike in May-June 1968, when the party launched a 'democratic' pétanque tournament under the patronage of J. Duclos.
- *l'Humanité* and *l'Humanité Dimanche* devote entire pages to football and racing results, reports on the Tour de France or the Olympics, and even the results of the National Lottery, in exactly the same style as any bourgeois newspaper.
- All this is theorised by the Communist Party's ideologues. Sport becomes 'part of mankind's cultural heritage', the Olympics are described as 'the greatest cultural spectacle of all time', and as 'a great disinterested festival of youth'.
- To give credibility to the policy of 'advanced democracy' and democratic sport, the PCF holds up the example of E. Germany, the sporting garrison. According to the PCF, the number of people

taking part, the para-military mobilisation of the population for sport in the work-places, residential areas and colleges and the number of medals won and records broken are symbols of the success of 'socialist' sport. This is the model which the PCF seeks to establish in France under an 'advanced democracy'.

(3) *The Olympics and Regimentation*

Modern sport is subjected to the policies of the bourgeois state apparatus. It helps to reproduce and inculcate the general themes of bourgeois ideology: respect for hierarchy, individual advancement, the self-made man, business values, selection, the cult of the leader, the cult of effort and repressive morality. The very modes of operation of sport are such as to contribute to the development of an ideology that pervades the mass media: the search for maximum output, the need for training and competition, the obsession with winning and breaking records, the star system and so on.

In the context of international competition for sports prestige and in order to serve its diplomatic and military interests, the state does everything to encourage nationalism and chauvinism in sport. Victories or successes on the part of national athletes are presented as successes for the government of the day and the athletes are decorated for their services, invited to government receptions and the like.

According to Coubertin the aim of the Olympic ideal is to achieve 'reconciliation of all races'. This is far from reality.
– Black athletes are excluded from 'racially pure' teams in South Africa.
– Racial minorities are segregated within the teams themselves, as in the case of the Black Americans in the Mexico Olympic village.
– The colonialist powers use sportsmen and women from their colonies to serve their national sports effort.

It is also worth recalling the topical example of the Berlin Olympics, which took place in the midst of anti-Jewish repression. Despite this 'memory', the Olympics have retained a number of racist features, typified by the senile crab Brundage, who has not forgotten his pre-war pro-Nazi past.

In strong states, whether military, bonapartist or fascist (Hitler,

Franco, Pétain, de Gaulle), the bourgeoisie has always operated a policy of militarisation and regimentation of youth, through sport and through youth organisations linked to sport or to the army (the scouts, the Hitler youth, the 'Chantiers de la jeunesse' under Pétain etc.).

And finally all bourgeois institutions – schools, family, army, church etc. – openly recommend sport as a way of turning young people away from sexual activity and sexual pleasure. Sport is seen as a repressive antidote to adolescents' sex drives. 'Sport, not love,' is the general slogan of all these institutions, which seek to channel sexual energy in the direction of sporting effort and submission to authority.

At the Olympics, where men and women have always been segregated, the cult of the virile strength of the muscle-bound male is put over as a model for young people as a whole to follow.

The spectacle of sport, which has become the staple diet of the mass media, is a powerful means of propaganda for de-politicising the alienated masses. Sport is an opiate of the people, in that it turns workers away from their real political preoccupations which are submerged under the flood of sports results, racing results, the national lottery and trivial news items. Sports fetishism and ideology enable the ruling class to camouflage political conflicts and the class struggle.

The *Ecole Emancipée* could not let the Munich games go by without reacting. These Games fit into the present political situation on a world scale, serving to camouflage the class struggle. They are the most extreme example of the moronic sports spectacle, the purpose of which is to hammer obedience to the bourgeois order into the heads of young people and the oppressed masses generally.

Faithful to our tradition of proletarian internationalism, the *Ecole Emancipée* calls on workers the world over to condemn the masquerade of the Olympics and develop the class struggle against their own bourgeoisie.

The *Ecole Emancipée*, July 1972.

Draft Appeal for the Setting Up of an Anti-Olympic Committee*

Soon, four years will have gone by since the 1972 Olympics were staged in Munich. The Munich Games were a huge institutional flop, which demonstrated that what is repressed always comes back up to the surface. The endless series of incidents, blunders, hesitations, fumblings and the prevailing atmosphere of guilt and bad conscience were all sure signs that the institution of sport had entered a deep crisis.

We recall the 'pirate' action of Black Americans raising clenched fists during the 400 metres medal ceremony; the leaflet distributed in favour of a united Ireland; the petition against the Vietnam war started by American athletes; and above all the terrorist action by a Palestinian *Black September* commando (whatever we may think of this intervention from other points of view). All these intrusions hit the institution of sport hard, if indirectly, unmasking the mystificatory Olympic verbiage in practice. For while Brundage, the President of the International Olympic Committee, was making speeches about 'peace, peace-making, mutual understanding between men and human development', everyday reality was somewhat different.

– US imperialism was devastating Indochina,
– the CIA was manoeuvring in various parts of the world against oppressed peoples,
– the Soviet bureaucracy continued to occupy Czechoslovakia with the troops of the Warsaw pact and the political police,
– oppositionists in the USSR were being tortured in 're-education' camps and psychiatric hospitals,
– the military and police 'gorillas' of Latin America were hunting

*This draft appeal first appeared in *Quel Corps?* No. 3 (November-December 1975).

down revolutionary worker militants as in the Trelew massacre, – the Zionist state of Israel continued to deprive the Palestinian people of their national rights . . .

The Munich Games was a conscience-salving exercise for a complacent bourgeoisie, in which imperialism provided the starving masses of the oppressed colonial countries with the spectacle of its police apparatus supervising a publicity circus for multi-national companies.

The Games were intended to get the peoples of the world and the international proletariat to forget the reality of class oppression, the reality of torture under police states, and the reality of under-development designed to boost the profits of monopolistic financial powers.

The Games were meant to be an example of the sacrosanct 'peaceful coexistence between states with different social systems', as the official formula goes. The ideological justification of the Olympics is provided by this notion of peaceful coexistence between the great imperialist powers and the so-called 'socialist' countries. According to this counter-revolutionary conception, countries are supposed to engage in 'dialogue', through the intermediary of their athletes, with the purpose of proving on one side, the superiority of 'the American way of life', and on the other, the joys of 'cybernetic socialism'.

Thus in 1972 radicalised young people and progressive intellectuals started to develop a challenge to competitive sport. On the initiative of the *Ecole Emancipée*, the majority of the organisations of the French far-left took part in the setting up of a national Anti-Olympic Committee. The aim of the committee was to expose the 'great universal youth festival' and the 'brotherhood between peoples' it was supposed to bring about as an imperialist masquerade. Although the committee only represented a minority current of opinion, it succeeded in fulfilling two basic tasks. First of all it provided a concrete illustration of proletarian internationalism in an area which the bourgeoisie and reformists have always regarded as, in the last analysis, politically neutral. And secondly it uncovered the mechanisms of sport intended for mass consumption, which has become a new opiate of the people.

At the same time anti-Olympic committees were set up in Italy and Germany. The German committee brought the challenge to the Games to the Olympics site itself, showing that a whole number of young people were no longer prepared to swallow the lies about the 'Olympic truce' and the 'democratic aims' of the Games, peddled by the illusion merchants. There were several street demonstrations during the opening ceremonies, several protest actions were held in the course of the competitions, and meetings and local forums were organised, showing that the time had come for a fundamental reappraisal of the Olympics.

Now the ruling classes are getting ready for a re-run of the Olympic tragi-comedy. In July 1976, the Games will be staged in Montreal. The Canadian bourgeoisie is determined to avoid another Munich, so they are making sure they are prepared.

— 500 trade union militants have been suspended from the labour force working on the facilities for the Games;

— the construction sites are permanently guarded by the notorious private security firm, Pinkerton;

— there have been an increasing number of raids and searches in the homes of far-left militants ('What will you be doing in July 1976?');

— the concentration of repressive forces is expected to be the biggest in the history of the Games. Several thousand soldiers of the Canadian Army, the Montreal police, the Quebec security force, the anti-terrorist units of the Royal Canadian police force, the Canadian and American secret services, the FBI and the CIA will all be on duty at the rites of the 'Olympic religion', in Coubertin's words . . .

All this, because the Olympic Games today represents too much of a godsend for the bourgeoisies and bureaucracies of the world. Their interest in the Games is of three kinds:

Political . . .

The ideology of the Olympic movement, and of sport in general, assists the stabilisation of the social status quo and the established order. Sport brings order . . . but at the same time sport can only function if order is maintained. Thus the ideology of sport provides a 'democratic' smokescreen for the tendency for strong states to become police states. The massive deployment of military and police forces is inherent to the staging of national or international sports meetings. Just think of the 1,500 Swedish cops needed to protect the Davis cup team sent by the torturer Pinochet to Olaf

Palme's social democratic paradise. Such operations have the purpose of getting people used to the large scale police manoeuvres so dear to Interior Ministers' hearts. Indeed what could be more natural than for the cops to be there to protect the regular and orderly functioning of sports contests?

On the internal front, the Games enable the various states involved to build a 'holy alliance' around the national teams entrusted with the task of defending the country's colours. There are expected to be two million spectators in Montreal, and the Games will be seen by one billion viewers on television. 6,500 journalists representing 70 radio stations and 100 national and international TV networks will be there to cover the events. Thus through the mass media, bourgeoisie and bureaucracy alike seek to stuff the masses with sports results, hoping that they will forget the everyday reality of exploitation and class struggle. By getting the masses to acclaim the exploits of the 'gods of the stadium', the ruling classes make maximum use of the function of the Games as a diversion from the class struggle and an antidote to political action.

And then on the external front, the Olympics offer a whole number of strategic, military and diplomatic advantages. All the agencies of imperialism, the UN, UNESCO and the rest, will be able to explain to the oppressed peoples that they must set their struggles on one side for the duration of the 'truce', that they must respect the rules of sportsmanship in their daily confrontations with the armed bands of capital. Amidst the nationalist hysteria which the Olympic duels will inevitably unleash, the bourgeoisie will be able to conceal its policy of plunder and pillage of the resources of the peoples of the third world.

Economic

The Olympics constitute a vast commercial circus which brings in considerable profits for the organisers and the public and private promotors who provide the finance.

– For the Olympics, international finance capital invests in the most sophisticated electronic equipment (which is incidentally supplied by the same firms that supply military equipment). Thus for example, in 1976, the Olympic torch will be carried from Mount Olympus to Montreal by laser beam!

– In Canada there is an inflation rate of 10 per cent per year, yet inflation in the construction sector has reached 46 per cent over the last two and a half years.

– The Olympics give rise to a vast urban development operation. A new airport, 'Mirabel', is being built, together with a new motorway network, nine underground stations, a 10,000 place Olympic village and new sports facilities, for a cost of 650 million dollars, which is to be added to the 73 million dollar budget of the Organisation Committee.

– The Olympics are the scene of a veritable financial jamboree with the sale of 'Olympic special' national lottery tickets bringing in 30 million dollars a year and continuing after the Olympics are over, the sale of television rights, the European retransmission rights alone fetching 10 million dollars, the issuing of Olympic coins, Olympic stamps, the sale of licences for the commercial use of the Olympic emblem, Olympic souvenirs . . . the list is endless.

By organising the sports spectacle, capital puts over its most extravagant image throughout a world in which whole populations suffer from illiteracy, famine and poverty. Even in Montreal itself they have had to put up multi-coloured fences to hide some 100,000 slum dwellings.

Ideological

Bourgeois institutions as a whole will take advantage of the mental fog that will descend on the masses as they are gripped by the orgy of superhuman records and exploits.

All the channels of information and indoctrination will inject the masses with a high concentration of ruling class ideology. All the bourgeois values will be hysterically hammered home: individualism, aggression, virility, the myth of the superman, male chauvinism, the cult of the strongman, the myth of indefinite progress, the justification of competition, industrial efficiency, sado-masochism and so on. The hack press will submerge the working class in chauvinist, racist, aggressive, condescending and idiotic commentaries. Industrial-scale brain-washing will break all records.

In such a situation, revolutionaries have three tasks:
(a) The first is to develop a critique of bourgeois ideology in the specific field of sport – an ideology which is particularly virulent be-

cause sport is not perceived for what it is. Revolutionaries cannot and must not leave a single area of everyday life open to the influence of the bourgeoisie. The task of a revolutionary communist critique of sport is to uncover the class roots of the practice of sport and to trace the mechanisms by means of which the opiate of sport is employed in the cultural colonisation of the working class.

(b) The second task is to carry out anti-Olympic propaganda and agitation on the basis of the principles of proletarian internationalism. International working class solidarity is necessary not only for defensive tasks but equally for offensive action against imperialist manoeuvres. Such activity also provides useful opportunities to expose the machinations of bourgeois states against the oppressed classes and peoples. An international revolutionary campaign will not be wasted at a time when the mass of workers are being submitted to intensive bourgeois propaganda on the beaches and in holiday resorts.

(c) The final task is to develop a conception of the kind of bodily activity and physical education we want to see in the socialist society we wish to build. Faced with the reformist and stalinist caricatures of sport, we have to be able to propose revolutionary alternatives to current practice. The critique of sport gives us the chance to make known to a mass audience our conceptions of the education of the body under a socialist system. In this field as in others we have to challenge the domination of the traditional organisations of the working class. As Gramsci said in essence, bourgeois ideology has to be fought all along the line. The cultural revolution starts here and now, in the course of the struggles of youth and of the working class for another life in another society.

Quel Corps? September 1975.

Twenty Theses on Sport*

I The Birth of Modern Capitalist Sport

1 While it is true that humanity has always engaged in physical exercise for playful, competitive, utilitarian or military purposes – collective games, hunting, ritual physical exercises etc. – it is false to claim that sport is 'as old as the hills' or 'part of the heritage of humanity'. *Such mystical conceptions present sport ahistorically, as a transcendent entity, over and above historical periods and modes of production.*

2 Sport as an *institution* is the product of a historical turning point. Sport appeared in England, the birthplace of the capitalist mode of production, at the beginning of the modern industrial epoch. From the start, sport was not a homogenous institution but a *class practice*. Sport meant different things for different social classes. While for the bourgeoisie sport was conceived as a leisure pursuit and a form of distraction, the proletariat experienced the need for sport as a means of physical recuperation. This explains why the workers' movement has since its inception adopted the demand for the right to sport along with the right to work, and has fought for this demand within the struggle for the reduction of working hours.

3 Britain exported her main forms of sporting practices along with her commodities and gun-boats, to India, Southern Africa etc. *The birth of world sport parallels the consolidation of imperialism.* The great international sports federations were set up at the turn of the century around the time of the first World War, at the same time as the other great supra-national organisations such as

*First appeared in *Quel Corps?* No. 1 (April-May 1975).

the League of Nations. Today the international authorities of world sport are completely integrated into the mechanisms of imperialism.

4 Sport is a consequence of the level of development of the productive forces under capitalism. It is a product of the reduction of working hours, of urbanisation and the modernisation of the means of transport. Sport *itself* turns the body into an instrument which it helps to integrate into the complex system of productive forces. Such a relative development of the productive forces is in *stark contrast to the chronic under-development of physical potential* in the countries dominated by imperialism, reflected in malnutrition, deformities and so on.

5 This development of physical potential through sport has taken place in the context of bourgeois production relations. As a class institution, sport reproduces these production relations in an ideological form. In this respect sport has become *state monopoly sport,* totally controlled by the centralised state apparatus. This is why any perspective of reform is illusory. Sport must be smashed, like the state machine.

6 *The institution of sport is geared into the mechanisms of the capitalist system.* Sports clubs operate like firms competing on the sports market. The capitalists of sport appropriate players and athletes who thus become their wage labourers. Within the clubs, the class struggle takes on the specific form of a struggle between the suppliers of capital and the suppliers of performances. The relations between the managements and sportsmen are *wage relations,* with all that this implies: exploitaton of the capacity to produce performances, sports trade unionism etc.

7 The competitive sportsman is a *new type of worker* who sells his labour power – that is to say his ability to produce a spectacle that draws the crowds – to an employer. The exchange value of his labour power, governed by the law of supply and demand on the market, is determined by the labour time socially necessary for its production. Amateurism ceased to exist a long time ago. All top-level sportsmen are professional performers in the muscle show. They are also very often advertising 'sandwich-board' men.

8 The sports system is thus an integral part of the capitalist mode of production, constituting a specific sector within the

capitalist division of labour. Economic trusts, banks and monopolies have taken over the financial side of sporting activity, which has become a prized source of capitalist profits. Competition for these profits is spurred on by the profits of competition. Hence the number of sports competitions is stepped up in order to speed up the circulation of sports capital and the production of surplus value.

9 Mass spectator sport is a vast capitalist enterprise within the entertainments industry – hence part of the tertiary sector. The commercialisation of sport operates on four principal levels:
– the establishment of a sports products, goods and services industry – winter sports, tourism, the equipment market etc.,
– the development of spectator sport as a base for advertising
– the tapping of citizens' (and particularly workers') resources to swell the coffers of the stadiums,
– likewise, for the sports betting industry – racing, the pools etc.
The sports system is thus an integral part of a massive monetary circulation network, which means that any hope of 'cleaning up sport' financially speaking is an illusion.

10 The numerous and frequent scandals affecting the sports system – fraud, tax evasion, extortion, illegal transfers, bankruptcies and various shady schemes – are a specific reflection of the crisis of state monopoly capitalism and its disintegration through inflation, unemployment etc. This crisis will inevitably give rise to struggles on the part of the practitioners and consumers of sport, in which we will have to intervene.

11 International economic competition between imperialist and bureaucratic state focusses around the struggle over who will organise major international sports meetings such as the Olympics. Such events require considerable capital investments and contribute to regional or national economic development, through the opening up of markets, the provision of facilities etc. *The growing scale of the Olympics reflects the pressure of the economic, political, diplomatic and military combines which are set up to profit from them.*

II The Ideological Functions of Sport

1 *Sport has the function of justifying the established order.* Sport is a *positivist system* and as such always plays an integrating and never an oppositional role. This justificatory function flows from sport's typically optimistic ideology of indefinite, linear progress. Progress can only lead to *improvement,* and hence any system which brings it about must be intrinsically good. Whether in the East or in the West, sport everywhere aims to get the masses to *acclaim* the established socio-political system as a whole. Sport thus functions as a *justification* of the joys of the 'American way of life' or the 'socialist system'.

2 *Sport is a stabilising factor for the existing system:* – by conning people into identifying with the champions, sport has a de-politicising effect. The champions are the positive heroes of the system: those who by their own efforts and labours have succeeded in climbing the rungs of the social ladder. They justify and reinforce the social hierarchy. By holding out this perspective of salvation via a parallel hierarchy, sport sows illusions in the possibility of social advancement.
– by camouflaging the class struggle, sport operates in every social formation in the world as a new type of opiate of the people. Social conflicts and the class struggle are acted out metaphorically in individual or collective muscular contests (Cf. the ideology of sportsmanship);
– by the rationalisation of the general myths of bourgeois society:
* economic competition is presented metaphysically as an eternal given, whose playful representation is sport;
* the hierarchy of sport which is maintained by the classification of physical performances assists the perpetuation of the hierarchic structure of capitalist production relations;
* social inequalities are reproduced in exaggerated form within sport, but are masked by the pretence of equality between competitors – everyone starts off under the same conditions;
– by stabilising itself as an ideological bloc, distilling the ideology of its own apparatus – hierarchy, selection, training, competition, bureaucracy, formalism etc. These ideological values are embodied in the ritualistic practices of protocol, ceremonial etc. which serve to maintain the consistency and unity of the institution of sport.

3 *Sport is a practical application of the ideology of 'peaceful co-existence between states with different social systems'.* This status quo is strengthened by the integration of sports organisations into the institutions of imperialism – The World Health Bureau, the International Trade Union Bureau, UN, UNESCO etc. The Olympic ideology of the truce, of brotherhood and peace is an application of the notion of peaceful coexistence within sport. For a period of a month the struggles of oppressed classes and nations is supposed to come to a halt while they gaze at the 'Gods of the stadium'. This ideology is constantly being contradicted by the reality of international conflicts. Thus the history of the Olympics has al-ways been punctuated by the sound of gun-boats and struggles. In 1956 there was the Franco-British Suez expedition against Nasser's Egypt and the bloody repression of the Hungarian workers' councils by Khruschev's tanks. In 1968 the military junta of fascist Diaz Ordaz shot down several hundred revolutionary students in the Square of the Three Cultures, Mexico City. And then in Munich in 1972 the Games were held to a background of US imperialism bombing North Vietnam with napalm and anti-personnel bombs. Here we have the reality behind the 'Olympic peace', the so-called oasis of brotherhood which is really nothing but class collaboration between oppressors and oppressed.

4 *Sport is a way of preparing labour-power for capitalist industrial labour:*
– instilling into people, early in life, the principle of maximum output and the productivity of the organism;
– adapting the body to the principles of mechanised labour. Sport employs the same techniques in this respect as industry – the divi-sion of labour, the encouragement of automatic reflexes, the for-malisation of all movements etc. Sport 'Taylorises' the body and inculcates a moral code based on effort and labour, thereby contributing to the perpetuation of the exploitation of the working class;
– appearing as politically neutral, sport encourages class colla-boration by illustrating the possibility of a reasonable dialogue between the participants (the 'two sides of industry'), under the supervision of an impartial referee (the state).

5 *Sport is a powerful factor of sexual repression.* In sport, the prevailing form of relation between individuals and their own

bodies is a sado-masochistic one: pleasure in painful effort – 'The more it hurts, the more it's doing you good!' Sport combats eroticism by de-sexing the muscular and sensory apparatus. Specifically sexual pleasure is replaced with pleasure in painful movement. Sport operates as an antidote to sexual desire by channelling it into sporting effort. This explains the efforts of educationalists to get adolescents to practice sport, thus combating masturbation and what are judged to be 'premature' sexual relations. The repressive and unhealthy homosexual atmosphere – the showers, changing rooms, 'virile' friendships etc. pervading sport (as in the army) – is the reflection of the permanent struggle to impose a well-regulated, genital sexuality through sport, capable of adapting to bourgeois monogamy.

6   Sport is a means of militarising and regimenting youth.
– Hitler, Mussolini, Franco, Pétain and de Gaulle all used or use sport to regiment youth in their efforts to put out the flame of proletarian revolution. Sport serves this purpose by developing *a standardised image of the body*, regulating the way the adolescent relates to his or her own body and seeking to establish the ideology of the body as a sort of automated machine. As a 'character school', sport creates authoritarian, aggressive, narcissistic and obedient character types, preparing young people for integration into society and training them to operate as alienated machines on the capitalist market.
– Sport contributes to the militarisation of youth with the aim of reinforcing the nation's military potential and preparing for imperialist war. It is worth noting that sport is held in high regard in the army and that the pioneers of physical and sports education were soldiers – Amoros, Baden-Powell, Hebert *et al.*

7   *The sports spectacle reinforces the commodity spectacle, by presenting, as a spectacle, human commodities.*
– The spectacle of sport magnetises enormous crowds – up to a million 'live' and up to a billion via television. As the biggest mass spectacle, sport operates as a sort of catharsis machine, an apparatus for transforming aggressive drives. Instead of expressing themselves in the class struggle, these drives are absorbed, diverted and neutralised in the sporting spectacle. Sport regulates and socialises aggression by providing permitted models of violence. Violence is thus codified, enabling all forms of direct action to be

out-lawed (put the shot instead of throwing bricks). So sport channels the energies of the masses in the direction of the established order.

– The spectacle of sport treats the masses as morons. Most of the mass media are saturated with trivial stories and futile sporting incidents (Kopas' knee, Bobet's boil etc.). The purpose of these meaningless dramas is to fill the masses' minds with trivia to prevent them thinking about political struggle.

– The spectacle of sport operates in such a way as to reduce the crowds, who provide it with 'cheering machines', to an undifferentiated mass in the stadiums, and in this respect it contributes to a process of emotional fascistification, reflected in march pasts, the profusion of flags, medal ceremonies, national anthems, salutes etc. The surrounding of sports events with ostentatiously displayed security forces has the purpose of getting people used to their presence. The law and order of sport depends on maintaining law and order in general, and *vice versa*.

8   Within the totality of bourgeois superstructures sport has a special place at the intersection of three specific elements:
– the everyday institutionalisation of the body,
– the education system,
– the spectacle of sport and the mass media.
This accounts for the complexity and contradictory character of the institution of sport. In this respect, as in others, sport is affected by class contradictions and plays an important role in the class struggle.

9   Women are enslaved by the patriarchal structure of capitalist society. As a vector of ruling class ideology, sport reproduces this slavery and provides it with a justification in terms of the 'naturalness' of the individual. Sport aims to get women to be content with their subservient function.
– it institutionalises sex differences – certain events do not exist for women – weightlifting, boxing, pole-vault etc.
– it structures women's bodies by systematising specifically feminine myths into various sporting activities:
– swimming, water ballet: the woman as siren or water nymph.
– gymnastics, sprinting, high-jump: feline suppleness.
– skating, ice dancing: grace and visual beauty.
– putting the shot, throwing the hammer, cycling etc.: the

serious, active, hard-working woman – the homely creature.

The fact that women are tending to practice sports hitherto restricted to men (which are incidentally the most popular sports – football, rugby and so on) does not open up any perspective for their liberation, in that it identifies liberation with the emulation of men and hence perpetuates the patriarchal system. This is a sort of half-measure, leading via an apparently different form of alienation back to the same. It underlines the conception that discrimination is justified by natural difference and thus operates within the logic of the régime. The only true possibility of liberation is offered by the advent of communism.

These theses do not claim to be exhaustive. Their aim is to provide the basis for discussion, preliminary to the setting up of a bigger and more internationally based anti-Olympic committee than the one which emerged at the time of the Munich Olympics.

Quel Corps? seeks to aid all comrades, all trade union and political organisations to develop the necessary anti-Olympic activity and expose the Games for the masquerade they are. The Olympics serve to camouflage the class struggle. They are the highest expression of the moronic sports spectacle, hammering home the ideology of the ruling class. They are the most spectacular example of the repressive functions of the institution of sport which is a brake on the struggles of workers everywhere against their bourgeoisies and bureaucracies.

Quel Corps? February 1975.

Appeal for the Boycott of Argentina as Organiser of the Football World Cup

Will the Football World Cup, scheduled in Argentina in June 1978, take place amongst the concentration camps? Will the French Football team find itself playing just half a mile from the worst torture centre in the country? For that, in effect, is the distance which separates the *Rio Plate* stadium, where several of the World Cup matches should be played, from the *L'Escuela de Mecancia de la Marine* (The School for Marine Engineering), headquarters of the sinister *Grupo de Tareas 3-3*, a real Argentinian gestapo, made up of 314 soldiers and officers from the Marines. In the last two years of this organisation's existence, hundreds of men and women have been atrociously tortured there, burnt by blow-torches, sawn alive with an electric saw, skinned alive etc. It is also from the school of Marines that the helicopters take off to discard the mutilated bodies into the *Rio de la Plata* or the Atlantic.

In Argentina, for more than two years now, at least 8,000 people have been imprisoned, more often than not without any judicial procedure, and 15,000 have 'disappeared', according to the figures of Amnesty International. Moreover, the estimate for the numbers assassinated by the various state forces over the same period is between 8,000 and 10,000 people.

This we must never forget.

The Argentinian Military Junta, which is imposing by nazi methods a policy of unprecedented misery, has turned the World Cup into an affair of State. This is shown by the total mobilisation of the government at the head of the Sports organisations, and the omnipresent intervention of all the repressive organisations in the preparations for staging the World Cup. For the Junta, it is a question, on the one hand of restoring its tarnished international image, on the other of reinforcing its authority and cohesion internally. The tyrannical régime of General Videla has been directed, since the coup d'Etat of 24 March 1976, against the popular resistance; strikes, sabotage of production, slow-downs in the rhythm of production, demonstrations by the mothers of detainees and those who have 'disappeared', all these are mushrooming in response to hunger and arbitrary rule.

Given these conditions, can we give a blank cheque to the Argentinian Military Junta, which is turning the Football World Cup into a new instrument of its rule of terror? Can we tolerate the fact that hundreds of millions of dollars are being ladled out for a prestige operation while the buying power of workers has fallen in two years by 65 per cent, inflation has reached record proportions and 15 per cent of the Argentinian working class is hit with unemployment?

Can we accept that, as in Berlin for the 1936 Olympics, a sports gathering should take place which gives international backing to a fascist dictatorship?

Given the actual conditions of repression in Argentina, a boycott of this country as the organiser of the Football World Cup seems to us to be the only consistent and responsible reply.

There will be no football played in the space between the concentration camps and the torture chambers! The World Cup should not take place either in Argentina, or in any country where the Rights of Man are trampled upon.

The Committee for the Boycott of the Organisation by Argentina of the Football World Cup will multiply its initiatives to insure that the French team does not go to Argentina nor to any other country where democratic liberties are not respected, unless, between now and the start of the proceedings, the Junta
– frees all political prisoners, including those who have 'disappeared';
– re-establishes, completely and permanently, political freedoms, the right to form trade unions and democratic rights.

We call on all sportsmen and women, football fans, journalists, youth movements, political and trade union militants and their organisations, the Association for the Defence of Human Rights, all democrats and progressive people to join or to support the actions of the Committee for the Boycott of the Organisation by Argentina of the Football World Cup.

We would like to see, and will work towards a broad international coordination of initiatives for boycotting the organisation by Argentina of the World Cup, from Sweden, Spain, Italy, Holland, Scotland etc.